FREEDOM STAR

PROPHECIES THAT HEAL EARTH

As sent by
The Ascended Dear Ones
Saint Germain
El Morya
Sananda
Kuthumi
Kuan Yin
Mary
Nada
to

L O R I   A D A I L E   T O Y E

I AM
AMERICA

Seventh Ray Publishing
GOBEAN
Payson, Arizona
USA

"Send this message to the earth with love."

~LORD SANANDA
Sponsor Of The Transition

This reproduction is from an actual photograph taken on June 1, 1961, when Sananda appeared in visible tangible form and allowed this photograph to be taken. In 1963 he gave permission to Sister Thedra to use this image in conjunction with the work of The Association of Sananda and Sanat Kumara.

Copies of this Photograph and transcripts of his communications with Sister Thedra are available by writing to: A.S.S.K., 2675 West Hwy. 89-A, #454, Sedona, AZ 86336.

He also told Sister Thedra that although the image is valid, he is not limited by form of any kind, therefore he may take on any form or appearance necessary for the task at hand.

This book is lovingly dedicated to my first teachers of peaceful co-creation, my grandparents, Richard and Marie Hauger.

The purpose of this manual is to give guidelines for understanding the prophecies given by the Ascended Masters to Lori Adaile Toye.

All creation has a perspective that is attributed to the creation by the observer. Hence, the creation can only be understood or interpreted by the individual on a personal basis. This manual has a perspective of its own, and the view point is of the receiving prophet as she has come to understand the Masters' message to all of us. We are all called to this level of understanding as part of our evolution in a world community and as part of the personal evolution of our life contribution to the planet and its peoples.

We are all coming to this transition. No one is exempt. It touches old, young, rich, poor, all walks of life, all countries, all governments and all religious peoples. We are all in this together.

Lenard Toye
I AM America
April 18, 1995

prophesy

(prof´ e si) v., **1.** to speak as a mediator between God and man or in God's stead. **2.** to teach religious subjects or material.

prophecy

(prof´ e si) n., **1.** divinely inspired utterance. **2.** utterance under the inspiring influence of religious experience.
3. inspired declaration or revelation of the divine will including moral teaching by warning, consoling, exhorting, giving an example of fellowship with God and the like.

prophet

(prof´ it) n., **1.** One who speaks for another, especially for God. An inspired revealer, interpreter or spokesman. One who's office it is to deliver a message. **2.** A preacher who is distinguished from a priest. [1]

This small book presents earth changes as a teaching of prophecy. Received in four days, it's content was written with the inspired presence and spirit of the Ascended Masters. The word prophecy draws from its latin roots pro (forth) and phanai (to speak or to tell) and these prophecies boldly 'speak forth' and carry a message that you can hear if your ears are open.

This spiritual teaching is not a prediction or forecast of events; however, the backdrop of these changes seen through the lens of prophecy provides a powerful emotional word picture. It is this word picture and literal interpetation, that lays the foundation for its rich, spiritual message.

Open these pages and read the prophecies with an open mind and then an open heart. Don't get lost in faultlines and sinking lands; instead, take the time and the courage to peer beyond the illusion of the physical. Hopefully, then, you can extract the profound, yet simple teaching.

With peace and grace, I AM,

Lori Adaile Toye
January, 1993
Payson, Arizona

CONTENTS

"He hearkens after prophecies and dreams."

~ WILLIAM SHAKESPEARE

Also Known As Sir Francis Bacon,
Prophet Of The New Age

CHAPTER ONE

INTERPRETING PROPHECIES
VORTEXES AND PROPHECY
THE SIGNIFICANCE OF THE NUMBER 17 AND PROPHECY
VORTEX SYMBOLOGY & SACRED NUMEROLOGY
PYRAMIDS & VORTEXES
GOLDEN CITIES

Throughout history, the theory and concept of earth changes is ever-present. It is a story we find in all the major religions of our present day world.

Variations of earth changes stories and prophecies have been passed down from generation to generation through metaphoric and philosophic Greek myths to the shamanic stories of native peoples of all nations of the world. These truths travel through many religions and cultures, and is fascinating in its geo-dynamic, rich in its contribution to evolution and shocking when explored as reality.

It is this shock, or in gentler language, 'an awakening,' that we are attempting to address in this information. Prophecy is given to catalyze change, and is also a spiritual teaching which gives impetus to take action. Prophecy's definition is 'a divine inspiration.' However, the power of prophecy, is often found in its interpretation. The Oracles of Delphi were surrounded by five well studied and respected interpreters, each ready to announce their insights from the prophetess. Native American prophets traditionally used one or several steadfast translators who were knowledgeable of the ways of the people to whom they would deliver their prophet's message. In all instances of ancient prophecies, it was extremely rare for the prophet to interpret or publicly share the gift of prophecy. Prophecy was a spiritual gift, and traditionally was received through prayer and meditation, or, through ceremonial dreams and visions. The prophet was often considered to be a leader of his or her people, and assumed a position which gave insight and instruction to the priests. In this booklet, I have used an ancient Hebraic form of interpreting prophecies. The prophets of that age never allowed a prophecy to be heard, unless if it was scrutinized three times.

The Literal, The Metaphor & The Mystic Message

First, we will examine the prophecies from a literal point of view. To gain our first understanding, we will listen carefully and figuratively to what the prophecies are saying. This is an interesting process with detailed earth changes prophecies. Throughout the years I have matched many weather patterns and tectonic plate locations to earth changes prophecies. To a mind that needs scientific, empirical evidence to accept anything as 'real,' literal interpretative ability may be your gift.

For those who are intuitive, and 'feel' much better than 'know,' the second form of interpreting prophecy is for you. The second phase of interpreting prophecy with this method is known as the metaphor. Here, we find all literal description expanded into our hearts and we begin to feel the impact of its message intuitively. Metaphorically speaking prophecies are healing and creative and open our feminine energy.

At the third, and most exciting level of interpreting prophecy is the mystic meaning. It is here that the literal and metaphoric messages merge in an alchemical marriage to produce a new translation. That message is usually significantly simple and the hidden meaning revealed for universal application. In the back of this book I have extracted five mystic messages from over two thousand literal prophecies. The mystic message always gives a solution and shows us how we can use prophecy to heal our hearts and minds.

Whereas the literal and metaphorical meaning of earth changes prophecies opens our understanding to the process of the cleansing and purification of a planet and its peoples, it is the mystic message and inherent cosmology, that bridges prophecy into its rich spiritual vision. Pythagoras identified purification as a simple matter of assimilation. So, for all reasons apparent, we approach the cosmology of earth changes as a vision and opportunity to spiritually assimilate. This is a time of spiritual awakening, a time to 'assimilate,' or to digest spiritually, and become ONE with spirit.

"As above, so below," speaks the master teacher. Can heaven anchor on earth amidst wars, suffering and turmoil? According to the prophecies, the inevitable result hinges on humanity's choice. Will we annihilate ourselves in nuclear wars and destroy our bodies and our earth home through needless chemical pollution? Or, loosing her patience, will mother earth, simply roll over and shake us off her back? How much time is left and can we stop the tick of the doomsday clock?

The Time Is Now

The spiritual teachings contained in prophecies give us extra time in the countdown. They frequently state, "The Time Is Now." They state that this is a time to purify ourselves, first, so we can make careful choices. Or else, the earth mother will do this for us. If we want to avert or to lessen the prophesied earth changes, we must seek peace and harmony.

The prophecies state peace begins with each heart. As each person achieves this, then, we can join in mutual understanding of one another. If we are to obtain a United Brotherhood and Sisterhood on an earth freed from violence and ecological breakdowns we must begin today. It begins with our choices. The time is now.

In this prophecy, the earth is shown to go through tremendous upheaval and geophysical changes to be restored by the Law Of Grace and renamed the Star Of Freedom. This restoration is gloried by the power of our spiritual focus blending with the fruitful beauty of nature. Because nature and humanity are one, and cannot be disconnected, the new spiritual consciousness creates a new world. All the kingdoms of creation join in a natural harmony. In the prophecies, nature forms great cities of light to assist humanity's transition into the New Golden Age.

The Great White Lodge

This prophecy is brought through the Trans-Himalayan Brotherhood and Sisterhood, known as the Great White Lodge. The Great White (Light) Lodge is a fraternity of men and women dedicated to the universal spiritual upliftment of humanity. Their chief desire is to preserve the lost teachings and spirit of the ancient religions and philosophies of the world. They are pledged to protect against systematic assaults against individual and group freedoms that in-hibit the growth of self knowledge and personal choice. And, most importantly, their mission is to reawaken the dormant ethical and spiritual spark that has almost disappeared among the masses.

Commonly known as the Spiritual Hierarchy Of The Great White (Light) Brotherhood and Sisterhood, these Masters first presented this prophecy through a series of dreams starting in 1983. Through continual contact and guidance, the message from the dream evolved into the 1988 release of the **I AM America Earth Changes Prophecy Map for the United States**. In 1990, the prophecy expanded into the release of highly detailed earth changes prophecies for Central and South America. Through 1991 to 1994, these Masters of service had released the complete earth changes prophecies for the entire planet. Portions of these prophecies have been compiled and published in the **New World Atlas, Vol. 1, New World Atlas, Vol. 2**, and the **Freedom Star World Map of Earth Changes**.

Lord Sananda, Sponsor Of This Message

The earth changes message is sponsored by World Servant and Messenger, Sananda, (pictured in the beginning of this book). His guidance always teaches to, "Send this message to the earth with love." We now use the new name of Sananda, (as he is the former Jesus of the bygone Piscean Age), at his request. The new name is a higher frequency, and discards the church age name often identified with western imperialism, the abuse of native peoples and a scape goat whom so many foolishly cast their sins. It is said that the higher frequency Sananda, "Radiates the Dynamic Light centered personality through which the light energies now manifest in all that is beautiful, harmonious and peaceful." [2] He also takes the new name, so at this time, many more will begin to identify with the Christ energy as being within them and not separate or apart from them.

Lord Sananda works with a team of spiritual teachers who have organized part of their work into a series of three maps: First, the I AM America Map, containing information for the Americas. This land is referred as *the cup*, symbolizing the ability to bridge the physical world with spiritual energy. The Americas are sponsored by the spiritual teacher, Ascended Master Saint Germain. *(You can read the detailed prophecies for this map in New World Atlas, Vol. 1.)*

Second, the Greening Map, containing information for Eastern Europe, Russia, China, India, Japan and Australia. This land refers to *resurrection*, symbolizing the laws of ecological alchemy and humanity's ability to co-restore our planet as a garden through using the spiritual law of grace. The Greening Lands are sponsored by the Bodhisattva, Kuan Yin. *(You can read the detailed prophecies for this map in New World Atlas, Vol. 2)*

Third, is the Map Of Exchanges, containing information for Western Europe, The Middle East, Africa and the rising of New Lemuria. This land refers to the 'link' or 'connection' between the living planet and her peoples as we move into the Golden Age. The Map Of Exchanges is sponsored by Lady Nada, Goddess of Divine Justice and Healing for Humanity and the Ascended Masters El Morya and Kuthumi. This map is extremely important as it anchors the eighth, golden ray into co-creation. The sixth Elohim, (Elohims are benevolent, spiritual beings who focus the precipitation of created forms onto our planet), gracefully shifts its feminine counterpart, Pacifica, to serve with the individualized focus of the Golden Ray through eternal peace and fruitful desire. *(You can read the detailed prophecies for this map in New World Atlas, Vol. 3)*

The fifty-first golden city is served by the Archangel Crystiel Of The Eighth Ray, anchoring peace as eternal protection, healing and clarity for mankind.

VORTEXES AND PROPHECY

Each of the shaded areas on this map is where a vortex is prophesied to manifest. Numbered, to indicate the timing of their manifestation or activation, some of these vortexes are old vortexes that are shifting or changing locations. Some vortexes are entirely new. Said to be huge, these sacred energy sites are over 400 kilometers in diameter and over 200 miles high. These vortexes function very much like chakras do on the human body. They are points where the planet breathes, or takes energy in, or releases energy. Vortexes spin, clockwise to take in energy and counterclockwise to release energy.

The planet is very much a living and breathing conscious being. From this tradition, the Masters have named the earth, Beloved Babajeran.

Vortex Movement

You'll see the chakra or vortex energy movement many times in nature. Funnel like in appearance, devastating and powerful tornadoes, and simple dishwater going down the drain, mimic this basis energy movement. Scientifically, a vortex is a polarized motion body which creates it's own magnetic field, aligning molecular structures with phenomenal accuracy. "Nature has basically two types of motion. One is centripetal and the other centrifugal. Those motions have a definite geometrical pattern when they are generated by natural means. This geometrical form is called 'The Vortex.' A vortex is the three dimensional form by which all mediums like water, air, solids, electricity, magnetism, sound, light, etc. are generally maintained and dissipated. They give birth to and disperse our planet and all particles of matter." [3]

THE SIGNIFICANCE OF THE NUMBER 17 AND PROPHECY

Each of these maps contains 17 Golden City Vortexes, symbolizing the Star Of The Magi, and the birth of the Christ Consciousness throughout all of creation. Ancient Chaldean numerology refers to the 17 as the 8-pointed Star Of Venus as an image of love, peace and immortality. The seventeenth card of the tarot is the 'Stars,' and, according to tradition, symbolizes the divine powers of nature. Each of these maps unites to form a new planetary grid of 51 vortexes that the Masters call 'The Galactic Web'. It is this web, which births humankind from its present existence, to a new dimension of peaceful coexistence, united with the planet and all kingdoms of creation.

Research from twentieth century Russian scientists and the ancient creation story of the Sioux, merge together with prophecy to provide exciting insights on the number 17. In 1971, an article was published about three Moscow researchers, a historian, an engineer and an electrician. "Earth, they said, was not the simple spheroid it appeared to be. Hiding under the surface wrinkles of its body was a complex crystalline spirit being whose planetary regulating powers could be seen from space! The corners and edges of this etheric crystal appeared to map the nodes and paths of Earth's life energy; geological fault lines, anomalies (UFO sightings, visions, and cryptozoological beings), edges of tectonic plates, concentrations of biodiversity, centers of ancient civilizations and modern disasters, and the migratory paths of animals." [4]

The Creation Story Of The Siouxs

This spherical grid was also known to the Native American Siouxs as sixteen hoops. "In the beginning, all was hoops, within hoops, within hoops. These hoops were orbital paths: Earth's around the Sun, the Sun's around the center of the Milky Way, and the electron's around the nucleus. Everything, at every scale, had the same essential spherical shape and orbital path." [5] Their creation story wove fifteen hoops around the earth, and the sixteenth hoop became the icosahedron's orbital path! Creator then organizes the maze of hoops by calling out to the powers of the elements, "Come to the sixteen hoops, come to Earth!"

The same story of earth's creation grid is contained in Ascended Master teachings, however, it is referred to as the, "The Ring Map."

"It is the map of elemental life force for your planet. That which formerly served in the many ringed circle is now known as the Galactic Web."

New World Atlas, Volume One, *Cradleland, 3/10/90, Page 83*

Earth's Orbital Path Is Prophesied To Change

In the prophesied time of great change and birth for earth and her peoples, a seventeenth hoop is added. The crystalline shape of the earth is altered, and some physical changes occur. However, earth's orbital path is altered again, and the earth is prophesied to become like a star, violet in color, and enter into a new planetary system that circles around a new sun. The prophecy adds to the ancient story of creation, "Now... Come to the seventeen hoops, come to Freedom Star!"

"Unana, this that means Brotherhood, is the name of the new galaxy to be birthed. Freedom Star, as she shall be known, will be the first planet to enter into this void and circle around a great sun."

New World Atlas, Volume Two, *Unana, 4/18/93, page 41*

Researchers have proven that the intersections on the planetary grid are significant locations. Here is a partial list of some of the things you'll find on the present-day fifteen hoops, or crystalline corners on the earth's creation grid.

- The Great Pyramid at Giza
- Bermuda Triangle
- Easter Island Megaliths
- Findhorn
- Mouth of the Indus River, origin spot of all Hindu culture
- Nazca Plains, landing strip for ancient UFO's
- Great Zimbabwe, Africa's Stonehenge

New Civilizations, Animals and Plants

After the times of changes, the entire planetary grid will be altered to accommodate the new consciousness. Some of the new intersections are the prophesied locations of the 51 golden city vortexes. It is also important to note that the prophecies not only speak of earth changes and vibrational shifts in consciousness, but they also detail new cultures of people, animals and plants that will inhabit the earth. The prophecies speak about the future center of Brazil and, its location births a new civilization of people.

"Christed beings who are emerging at this time, those who are the leaders of the Golden Age. These beings are coming specifically from seven planets. The majority are indeed incarnating in this area; however, there are many scattered across the planet."

New World Atlas, Volume One, *Open Doors, 3/25/90, Page 99*

"These children, held within the divine concept of Beloved Mother Mary, are preparing their way to come into South America.

For the next ten years the forbearers of this 7th Manu will be incarnating within this swaddling cloth.

Before we make our plans for our global ascent, there is but one new Manu to come forth and these are the children of the Violet Ray.

These are children for the new galactic web. These children are an extension of you, your own blessed star seed."

New World Atlas, Volume Two, *Seventh Manu, 5/1/93, Pages 75-77*

During and after the times of changes, the prophecies state that we will also see many new forms of animals and plants.

"In this golden age there is a reseeding of sort, for these are seeds that have not been cast to the wind, but carefully planted, fertilized and cultivated. This is a field that comes, shall we say, in absolute harmony.

The time of regeneration comes to the planet and all restored in divine order. Here, over the blissful lands, new seeds are planted. From the planet Uranus will come a new, shall we say, species of birds. From the planet Venus comes, shall we say, new strains of flowers. From the planet Mercury will come, shall we say, new strains of grains and grass. From the planet Jupiter comes, shall we say, new strains of mammals."

New World Atlas, Volume Two, *Alchemy, 4/23/93, Page 55*

It is prophesied that the new civilizations, flora and fauna is birthed through the new planetary grid. Since the golden city vortexes are located on this new grid, it is important to know as much as we can about them, as their presence greatly affects the future and destiny of earth.

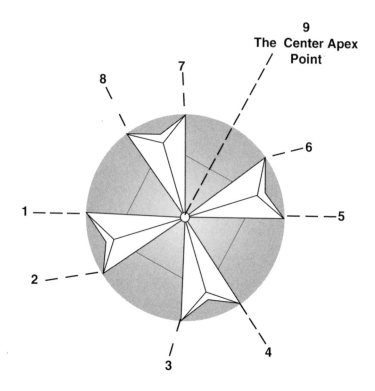

9
**The Center Apex
Point**

VORTEX SYMBOLOGY AND SACRED NUMEROLOGY

The visual shapes of these vortexes are a series of symbolic pyramids. The pyramid is the spiritual symbol of the descent and ascent of divine energy. The first shape is built on nine points, (nine is the number of divine man), and the second shape defines dimension by adding four more points, (four is the number of the earth representing her four elements, earth, air, fire and water). The first nine points represent the descent of divine power into the world. By adding four more points you achieve the number 13. Thirteen is the number of transformation and rebirth, (e.g., Twelve Apostles and the Christ; Twelve signs of the zodiac and the sun), thirteen also symbolizes leaving anything binding you and moves you into a new creation. This structure completes with the nine, and thirteen points sharing one continuous point, the apex. In the prophecies, the apex is the most powerful and significant location in the vortex. The sacred numerology leaves fourteen points, total, that reduce to the number 5. Five is known as the number of freedom and intelligent communication.

Additional insights on the number five, are given by Manly P. Hall, "The pentad - 5 - is the union of an odd and an even number (3 and 2). Among the Greeks, the pentagram was a sacred symbol of light, health, and vitality. It also symbolized the fifth element - ether - because it is free from the disturbances of the four lower elements. It is called equilibrium, because it divides the perfect number 10 into two equal parts.

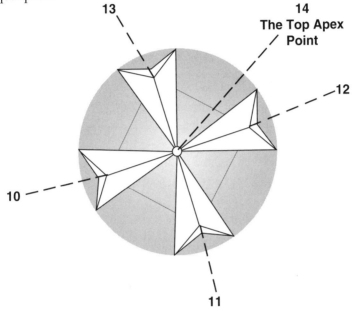

The pentad is symbolic of Nature, for when multiplied by itself it returns into itself, just as grains of wheat, starting in the form of seed, pass through Nature's processes and reproduce the seed of the wheat as the ultimate form of their own growth. Other numbers multiplied by themselves produce other numbers, but only 5 and 6 multiplied by themselves represent and retain their original number as the last figure in their products.

The pentad represents all the superior and inferior beings. It is sometimes referred to as the hierophant, or the priest of the Mysteries, because of its connection with the spiritual ethers, by means of which mystic development is attained. Keywords of the pentad are reconciliation, alternation, marriage, immortality, cordiality, providence and sound." [6]

The significance of the number five is easy to remember. Hold up your hand and count your four fingers, joined by one thumb. The simplicity of our hands, reminds us that we are four elements, (four fingers), joined by the fifth element, (the thumb), spirit.

Manly Hall expands this concept, "The tetrad (the elements) plus the monad (one) equals the pentad. The Pythagoreans taught that the elements of earth, fire, air and water were permeated by a substance called ether - the basis of vitality and life. Therefore, they chose the five-pointed star, or pentagram, as the symbol of vitality, health, and interpenetration." [7]

PYRAMIDS AND VORTEXES

The pyramids in Egypt represented to this ancient culture a new beginning and the pyramid-shaped hillock was used extensively in their agricultural practices. Each spring, the flooding Nile would recede and carefully cultivated hillocks would emerge, rich and fertile, ready for planting. Each small shaped hillock was symbolic of the reborn world.

Pyramids were also built, not as observatories or tombs, but as temples. The Great Pyramid was associated with Hermes, known as the Divine Illuminator, and worshipped through the planet, Mercury. (Mercury is also associated with the number, 17.) The pyramid temples were erected as physical displays of secret truths which are the foundation of all arts and sciences. "The twelve signs of the zodiac, like the Governors of the lower worlds, are symbolized by the twelve lines of the four triangles," writes Manly Hall, "The three main chambers of the Pyramid are related to the heart, the brain, and the generative system - the spiritual centers of the human constitution. The triangular form of the Pyramid also is similar to the posture assumed by the body during the ancient meditative exercises. The Mysteries taught that the divine energies from the gods descended upon the top of the Pyramid, which was likened to an inverted tree with its branches below and its roots at the apex. From this inverted tree the divine wisdom is disseminated by streaming down the diverging sides and radiating throughout the world." [8]

GOLDEN CITIES

Golden Cities, or sacred sites, have always been present upon the earth. Compared as chakras to the human body, their condition effects the overall health of the planet and they serve our holographic creation, anchoring divine energy on the planet. Vortexes have also been thought to be the location where major leilines, (leilines are electromagnetic meridians of the planet), cross. Thus, when you are inside a particular vortex you will have unusual experiences throughout your electromagnetic system. People have reported having increased psychic abilities, heightened spiritual awareness and increased health and well being when visiting or living in a Golden City. Most people following a path of spiritual communion with nature fall into Golden City vortexes naturally, mostly because they feel good! The energy is brighter, clearer and vibrant, and, the orgone, (life force), in vortexes is much more plentiful and charged.

Golden Cities Are Safe Places To Live In The Times Of Changes

Many good things can happen in Golden Cities. It is said, these are places where you can talk to the planet; caressing her with your good thought and prayer, and birthing new co-creations for humanity. Many Native Americans knew of such places and kept their locations well guarded for sacred ceremony and spiritual communion. Since the energy is always fine and high in such places, thought and intent manifests at a very high rate, allowing healing to come quickly. These places are great to hang out with friends and groups working together for global change. It is prophesied that in the future, intentional communities will grace every Golden City vortex.

Golden Cities are prophesied to be the first places on the planet, after the changes, where an evolution in human consciousness will begin. This evolutionary process will be based upon one principle, freedom. Freedom knows no separation in race, gender and economic status. With love and gentle grace; freedom manifests its own destiny to glorify beauty and cooperation in all creation and anchor heaven on earth.

The Ascended Masters have pledged their protection of these areas from any unbearable cataclysmic change. Each of these Golden Cities hold such clear and fine thought that they naturally express spiritual qualities as they pulse and vibrate. In this book, each of their qualities are listed, along with their cosmic sponsor; an Ascended Master, Beloved Elohim or Archangel. These sponsors pledge to serve humanity in these everpresent locations for twenty years. According to the prophecies, these spiritual teachers will manifest, and teach and heal the masses, gently and peacefully guiding human thought and feeling into the new millennium.

Along with the qualities manifesting in each golden city, a specific ray of light is prophesied to dominant in each of the fifty-one vortexes. Each color is also listed with the qualities. The seven rays of refracted white light have long expressed, in the most simple manner, God and creation as individualized perfection.

Golden Cities Of Other Times

In the last 2,000 year period, the planet held creative consciousness in 33 Golden City Vortexes. We know a few of these locations as:

- Mt. Shasta, California, USA
- The Great Pyramid At Giza, Egypt
- The Philippine Islands
- Vancouver Island, British Columbia, Canada
- Yucatan Peninsula, Mexico
- Philadelphia, Pennsylvania, USA
- The Azores of Portugal
- Lourdes, France
- Grand Teton, Wyoming, USA

As we begin to make our transitional shift in the expanding law of magnetic love, new Golden Cities are activated to hold a finer consciousness for the new planet known as Freedom Star.

Because the Golden City vortexes compose a sensitive global grid, all human interaction in these highly spiritual areas greatly affects the planetary pattern and the type of world that we live in. Presently, you can visit any Golden City vortex to send your healing energies. Your good thoughts and prayers will travel throughout this global matrix instantly. Your individual actions make a difference!

Beloved Tranquility, Elohim of the ray of ministration and peace proses:

> *"Peace is the healing of every distress.*
> *Peace is the feeling of God-happiness.*
> *Peace is the power of all God-control,*
> *Peace every hour will Victory hold!*
> *Peace is Love's gift to the children of men;*
> *Peace is forgiveness—again and again.*
> *Peace is the heart, the soul, and the mind.*
> *Peace fulfills God's great design!"* [9]

CHAPTER TWO

THE UNITED STATES / A LITERAL INTERPRETATION

The United States will be the first country to go through geophysical changes, and the first to recover, giving aid and support to the rest of the planet.

The first event is the sighting of a huge meteor coming to the planet, it's probable impact somewhere in the Nevada desert, upsetting faults and tectonic plates. This activates many volcanoes in the ring of fire, sending enormous amounts of dust and ash into the skies. Through this activity and subsequent global melting of the ice-caps, the oceanic currents are altered and the rotation of the planet on its axis shifts. This causes earthquakes on the western coast of the United States with California, Oregon and Washington state engulfed by waters to remain as only small islands. The Great Lakes burst with the overflow of waters by global warming and lower Lake Michigan drains into the Gulf of Mexico causing enormous erosion. The Mississippi River basin forms a huge bay.

The eastern coast of the United States is pummeled by hurricane winds and rains, and eventually, much of the coastline is broken into small islands by this activity. The northern tip of Maine is covered by ice through the action of shifting glaciers, and much of the Northeast is very cold, with a steady occurrence of moving and shifting glaciers.

The lower tip of Florida sinks due to earthquake and global warming activity and many of the nation's rivers swell beyond their present size. Many lakes disappear in seconds and rivers run backwards with the shifting of the poles. Huge fires erupt in the southwest and the Cascade mountain chains in Washington and Oregon continue their volcanic activity. All elements; Earth, Air, Fire and Water are involved in the great earth change of the United States.

During this time of earth change, there will be very few lands that will be unaffected. Massive groups of people migrate to inland lands, only to suffer more devastating earth changes. It seems as though it will never stop. More meteors come, and the night skies are filled with them. These changes are prophesied to begin around the year 1992 and close by the end of the year, 2009. After a period of restoration, the country rebuilds itself with the one third of its population that's left. In the year 2,200 AD, (or year 246 AF, Age of Spiritual Freedom), a new chain of mountains form on the east side of the present day Rocky Mountains.

☞ LITERALLY SPEAKING...

1989-FC, AN EARTHGRAZER STILL IN STRIKING DISTANCE

Did you know that in March of 1989, an asteroid came within a hairbreadth, (450,000 miles away), from colliding with the earth? It might be late breaking news now, but every 13 months, the asteroid known by astronomers as 1989-FC, passes by the earth and within 30 years scientists predict that it will collide either with the moon or the earth. That collision could be explosive, even though the asteroid's size is estimated between 500 and 1,000 feet in diameter. "Had it hit, says Bevan French, program scientist at NASA's Solar System Exploration Division, 1989-FC would have left a crater a half a mile deep and ten miles wide. The force of its impact would have equaled the explosive potential of 2,000 one-megaton hydrogen bombs, with fire storms and blast shocks leveling everything within a 50-mile radius. 'And that's the good news,' says French. 'If it hit the ocean, it would have produced tidal waves hundreds of feet high, probably wiping out most cities on the nearest coast." [10]

Here is the table that charts our rendezvous with 1989-FC:
September, 1995
October, 1996
November, 1997
December, 1998
January, 1999
February, 2000
March, 2001

CHAPTER THREE

THE UNITED STATES / THE METAPHOR

Americans have been entrusted with a great deal during the time of changes, and hold the concept of freedom for every living and conscious being upon planet earth.

Never before have such freedoms been enjoyed: freedom of expression, freedom from fear, freedom to choose who governs, and freedom to choose a life path that aligns to the heart's desire. This freedom is metaphored as the cup, and these people choose first, as even in the prophecy of earth changes, to apply their service to the world through their own experience and example.

This prophecy refers to the United States as a land of service and it is only through this principle will a great change come to the hearts of her inhabitants. The Masters' saying, "Love, in service, breathes the breath for all," is activated as each of us, realize that cooperation, is the thought and activity that unites us all.

The meteor represents recognizing the light in every heart as having value and honor. The meteor showers, later, represent all of those who have gone before us, honoring Divinity in all creation.

The ring of fire represents the flame of life in all creation, and the smoke and ash represent the activity of this flame.

The melting of the ice-caps represents how our hardness is melted and how easily life giving waters nurture our fruitful desire.

Sinking land represents letting go; forgiving and forgetting to allow a new creation.

High winds represent the great collective mind, and our own God intelligence that purifies and readies for co-creation with God. Breaking lands represent breaking man's own self imposed limitations breaking apart through purifying the mind and utilizing the power of thought.

Fire represents transmutation, and the new being we become through purification. Erratic movements of water represent our emotion and feeling world aligning to our hearts and preparing the path for our new journey in spirit.

Migrating peoples represent our unity, and oneness with all life. They also represent our yearning and longing to return to ONE law. We wish to commune and to be as ONE people, and willingly share in the law of love.

The new chain of mountains, represents our strength coming from the spiritual way of life, and how cooperation extends blessings and gifts to share.

❤ METAPHORICALLY SPEAKING...

WHY IS THERE A ROOSTER IN A WEATHER VANE?

Why is a rooster, and not a dove, in the middle of a weather vane? According to the ancient teachings, the rooster was the symbol of the male energy, and typified watchfulness and defense against the unexpected. The rooster was sometimes the emblem of the planet Mars and in the Samothracian Mysteries, was placed in the center of the four directions to represent the sun in midst of the four corners of creation.

On a deeper, metaphorical level, the rooster represented to the pagans the power of Mars in spiritual initiation; it's timeliness and purpose.

From the changes in our heart, comes a new vision for all of us. Lord Sananda saying, "If you have eyes to see and ears to hear, know now, you have hands to do!" teaches that we experience uprooting change so we learn to make empowering choices and take new action for co-creative world change. This new vision, or new myth, is present throughout this prophecy for the United States.

As our thought clears, our vision pierces beyond the veil, and we collectively choose grace and millennium principles to guide and direct our lives. As humanity begins to enter into the age of self-affirmation, great cities of light energy manifest to hold thought for God-given qualities. In our spiritual journey, we are inwardly guided to these great centers to further our development and restore our immortal being.

It is here, in these golden cities, that the prophecy states, Ascended Masters will reside, teaching and healing mankind for twenty years. The mystic message empowers us and states that we become and replace them as great servants and caretakers of life and creation. In this age of great bliss and peace, the prophecy states that time will stop and will no longer be needed.

These cities are shown in this prophecy to exist in the United States in these areas. According to the prophecy, we don't have to wait for geophysical changes to activate their great God Power for global healing influences.

In the United States, five cities are prophesied to manifest. They are:

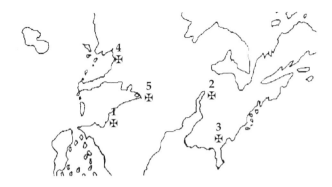

1. **GOBEAN**
   The Divine Will
   El Morya
   USA: Arizona, New Mexico
   Blue Ray

2. **MALTON**
   Fruition; Attainment;
   Self-Actualization
   Kuthumi
   USA: Illinois, Indiana, Kentucky
   Gold & Ruby Ray

3. **WAHANEE**
   Freedom and Justice For Humanity
   Saint Germain
   USA: Georgia, South Carolina
   Violet Ray

4. **SHALAHAH**
   Abundance and Healing For
   Humanity
   Sananda
   USA: Montana, Idaho, Washington
   Green Ray

5. **KLEHMA**
   Cooperation and Leadership
   Serapis Bey
   USA: Colorado, Nebraska, Kansas
   White Ray

Life in these golden cities is prophesied to be much different than the life we presently enjoy. Miracle healings, transfigurations and ascensions are common, everyday occurrences. Mankind is now called to a higher and divine purpose and each is readied to take a new position as a heavenly, cosmic being. In it's great transformation, our planet radiates and shines; sending its message of Freedom throughout the universe. Life from other planets responds. As the heart of the dove descends into the middle of the United States, The Great Star Of Freedom becomes home to many brothers and sisters of creation.

Great light of divine wisdom,
Stream forth to my being,
And through your right use,
Let me serve mankind and the planet.

▲ MYSTICALLY SPEAKING...

I CAN HEAL MYSELF AND THE PLANET THROUGH THE CHOICES I MAKE

Everyday we can avert cataclysmic global changes by shifting our consciousness and reflecting our commitment through our everyday choices. Then, we can start to fulfill the prophecies of peace. Each individual thought, desire and action contributes to the well being of our greater planetary family.

Through this collective critical mass, we can leverage consciousness to alter the outcome of many events. We can turn war into peace, famine into abundance, poverty into plenty. The choice is ours, everyday.

"Just as a scientist will work wonders out of various applications of the law of nature, a man who applies the laws of love with scientific precision can work greater wonders."
- Mahatma Ghandi

Ａs the earth changes begin to lift from the United States, a devastating earthquake erupts the west coast of Mexico, breaking Baja California into a series of erosive islands.

This major earth movement ripples down the Andes mountains, and the west coast of South America slides into the Pacific ocean. Aftershocks of this major tectonic movement tear the southern tip of South America, (Argentina), from the mainland, and this becomes one large island with many small islands surrounding it.

A large bay forms in the Amazon rain forest, and another near the city of Rio de Janeiro. After the southern tip of South America becomes islands, southern Uruguay sinks into the ocean and another bay opens the mainland, almost to Paraguay.

Of all the places in the world, South America is prophesied to undergo the least devastating of earth change. South America is said to be a land of destiny and held within the 'swaddling cloth of protection.'

New lands emerge: Resurrection Island off the west coast of Baja; White Dove Island off the coast of Peru, Bolivia and Argentina.

Around the year 2,200 another major shift of the tectonic plates create the Cooperation Mountains in the United States, and this sends another rippling effect throughout Central America. Huge mountains form a high ridge extending through Mexico, and down through the Central American countries of Guatemala, Honduras, Nicaragua, Costa Rica and Panama. As this ridge continues to rise, (Middle America Trench), it blocks off the ocean waters and forms a huge fresh water lake called the Lake Of Mirrors. (It is heart shaped.) The fresh water in this great lake comes from the melting of massive, ocean floating glaciers that become land locked. This major earth movement is as much as Atlantis will rise in this time period. The island of Cuba, Dominican Republic, Puerto Rico, The Virgin Islands and The Lesser Antilles Islands all rise to elevations of over 20,000 feet, forming the Silver Crystal Mountains and Pillar Peaks. From this enormous shift of rising lands, the Yucatan Peninsula, which was covered with water from the formation of the Bay of The Golden Sun, (Gulf of Mexico, draining of Great Lakes, Mississippi Basin), rises again, approximately in the year 2,242.

After the raising of Atlantis, a new continent makes its appearance in the Pacific Ocean, west of White Dove Island. Throughout the next 2,000 year period this new land will become inhabited by the children of the new age.

☞ LITERALLY SPEAKING...

EL NINO, WHY THE WEATHER IS DIFFERENT EVERYWHERE

El Nino is the warming of the equatorial Pacific Ocean, that is literally changing weather patterns across the globe. This mysterious warming, that happens around Christmas time is a phenomenon that normally develops every three to seven years. However, El Nino has returned three times in the past four years since 1991 with economically devastating effects. El Nino was obviously linked with the flooding of northern California in early 1995. But now, scientists have linked the global warming path of El Nino, to weakening plankton stirring trade winds on South America's west coast, seriously diminishing catches in fishermen's nets.

Rain is not the only outcome of El Nino. The drastic changes it brings to the gulf stream sometimes causes drought. The warming from its current, is said to be twice as strong as before. Similar patterns of warming have been noticed in the Indian Ocean, and could suppress summer monsoon rains relied upon by farmers.

It is now believed that the impact of El Ninos warming trends can last for 12 years. In 1982, the El Nino of the century set in motion and "The Pacific warming that struck devastated marine life and brought disastrous droughts or torrential rains to various parts of the world. Some scientists consider it the greatest disturbance of the ocean and atmosphere in recorded history." [11] This motion, known as a Rossby wave, is created when El Nino's warmth meets a continent and part of it bounces back. Scientists now theorize that a Rossby wave, possibly generated in 1982, played a major role in the 1993 flooding of the Mississippi.

There are still no clear answers why El Ninos are appearing in rapid succession, however, the buildup of carbon dioxide and greenhouse gases are highly suspected. The greenhouse effect may be disrupting the earth's system in such a manner that El Ninos are more likely to develop.

CHAPTER SIX

CENTRAL & SOUTH AMERICA / THE METAPHOR

The heart of change for South America comes from its prophesied name, The Motherland and Central America, The Cradleland. As these people once flourished as the highly developed Atlanteans, they rise again through destiny and sponsor the seventh manu, or next wave of incoming souls.

Its metaphor is strong and powerful, offering hope and grace for the children of the world, assuring a protective home through the practice of transmutation and compassion.

South America serves as the Great Mother, holding this immaculate conception and her womb, (the swaddling cloth), is an area of great nurturing and protection.

The opening of the Amazon represents the opening of the womb through birth; as all of humankind are birthed into creation to further glorify their divine source. Further openings of bays metaphor the sustenance given to the suckling or nursing infant, proving that Universal Law always provides all that we need for nourishment.

The new lands represent our emergence as divine beings and the small islands surrounding them represent shattered dreams as only the stepping stones that lead us to divine oneness.

The raising of the Cooperation Mountains between North and South America represents the umbilical cord or link between child and mother, and our duty as sponsors to help and support one another as we walk the path of world service.

The Lake of Mirrors represents duality, and the trials of life are overcome by practicing love in all things. Hence, the rising of high mountains, (Pillar Peaks), surrounding this heart shaped lake represents the activity of the law of love as light.   The results of this law, compassion, poise and transmutation, lift us above any trying circumstance.

♥ METAPHORICALLY SPEAKING...

BAD WEATHER...BLAME IT ON WARRING NATURE SPIRITS

The pagans, long ago, solved the problems of unpredictable weather by blaming it on the disagreements and warring attacks among the kingdoms of nature spirits. "When lightning struck a rock and splintered it, they believed that the salamanders were attacking the gnomes. As they could not attack one another on the plane of their own peculiar etheric essences, owing to the fact that there was no vibratory correspondence between the four ethers of which these kingdoms are composed, they had to attach through a common denominator, namely, the material substance of the physical universe over which they had a certain amount of power." [12]

The playgrounds of children have long been filled with weather storytelling, mirroring quite simply, common events of nature. Rain became the tears of angels; fog, their long tresses as they combed them; and, snowflakes, the flurry of their play, in a pillow fight.

M ary states in the message of change for the Motherland and Cradleland, "I AM a loving mother and I enfold you in my love and care." Here lies the mystic meaning of parental responsibility and how each and every one of us embodies the Cosmic Birther.

In Brazil, lies the Swaddling Cloth of Protection, its prophecy offering protection to new souls, incarnating on the planet to offer their great gifts of living forgiveness and grace. This manu will rise to rule the planet through these attributes, contributing to the everpresent harmony and peace on the Great Star Of Freedom. Even now, as these souls are incarnating, their gifts lie latent in poverty, abuse and confusion. This prophecy calls all of us to midwife their great birth! We are called to mother and cradle them. Hold your thought in prayer to the three vortexes of South America:

Love, from the heart of God,
Radiate my being with the presence of the Christ,
That I walk the path of truth.

These Golden City vortexes are sponsored by three Cosmic goddesses, Andeo, Braham and Tehekoa, known as the three sisters. They serve in the Motherland alongside the Great Divine Director. These vortexes are numbered in their awakening and activation:

30. **ANDEO**
*Consistency; City Of The
Feminine Aspect*
**The First Sister, Goddess Meru
Beloved Constance**
South America: Peru, Brazil
Pink & Gold Rays

31. **BRAHAM**
The Nurturer
The Second Sister
South America: Brazil
Pink Ray

32. **TEHEKOA**
Devotion
The Third Sister
South America: Argentina
Pink & Violet Rays

The Cradleland, or rising lands of Atlantis, cradle the new destiny of humankind, birthing a new reality and dimension of light and sound. Here, the prophecy asks us to consider laws of moral excellence and goodness. We are asked to synergize our efforts by aligning ourselves to the great heart of love. The golden cities are:

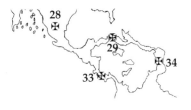

28. MARNERO
Virtue
Mary, (Twin Ray of Archangel Raphael)
Mexico: Santa Maria del Oro is the apex.
Green Ray

29. ASONEA
Alignment / Regeneration
Peter The Everlasting
Cuba: Santa Clara is the apex.
Yellow Ray

33. CROTESE
Heart Of Love / Divinity
Paul
Central America: Costa Rica, Panama
Pink Ray

34. JEHOA
Acts Of Love / Compassion / Gratitude
Kuan Yin
New Atlantis: The Island of St. Lucia is on the eastern side of this vortex. Since most of this land is prophesied to raise in the earth changes, much of the golden city is now anchored over waters 62° longitude and 14° latitude.
Violet Ray

▲ MYSTICALLY SPEAKING...
PARENTAL RESPONSIBILITY IS PLANETARY RESPONSIBILITY
"We are the custodians of the future of the Earth...Unless we check the rapacious exploitations of our Earth and protect it, we have endangered the future of our children and our children's children."
-Margaret Mead

CHAPTER EIGHT

CANADA / A LITERAL INTERPRETATION

The earth changes in Canada are simultaneous with the United States; they are lands united in their destiny of service to mankind.

Canada is known as the Land Of Creation, blessed with great abundance and relatively few earth changes occur during the transition.

The first event for Canadian earth changes is an earthquake in British Columbia, submerging the upper portion of Vancouver Island and the western coastline. A larger bay forms in northern British Columbia and the southern Yukon, forming a new coastline that is very jagged with amazingly high cliffs that drop off at 2,000 feet.

Global warming extremely effects Canada, with much water and disappearing northern lands. New islands form off the coast of Greenland, and the climate shifts to a warmer, more stable environment for agriculture. As Greenland thaws, she is shown to be five separate lands now divided by abundant rivers and lakes. Much of the Northern Territory disappears in the global warming, leaving a series of islands with the Hudson Bay doubled in size.

Several new seas are formed: The Abundant Sea, near Greenland; The Diamond Sea, near the new islands of the Northern Territory; The Sea Of Ellipse, near Alaska and British Columbia.

The province of Saskatchewan is hardly affected by the earth changes, and becomes a haven for many people during the times of changes, providing food for the Americas and gains a reputation as a 'bread basket.' Lake Winnipeg drains into an underground aquifer, and during this earth change, the city of Winnipeg floods. According to the prophecy, this could occur as early as 1998.

The Hudson Bay, (renamed Bay of Deliverance), extends south to newly formed Unity Lake, (the Great Lakes become one large lake), and the city of Ottawa is split in two by flooding rivers. During the shift of the poles, many rivers run in opposite directions, including the St. Lawrence river. Widening to four times its present day size, the St. Lawrence river flows into the Great Lakes region, and is renamed The Great River. Glaciers and ice covers the city of Quebec for 250 years, but Montreal's climate remains habitable. Lake Ontario drains to the south, (into upper New York state), and because of this devastating change, the city of Toronto is abandoned.

In the year 2,200, the Cooperation Mountains rise in the United States and extend into Canada, their peaks transforming the face of the province of Alberta, as far north to Edmonton.

☞ LITERALLY SPEAKING...

IF IT MELTS... IT WOULD BE THE NORTH POLE, NOT THE SOUTH

The Earth's heating system is fascinating. It works on basically two premises, first, radiation from the sun and, second, heat transport via the atmosphere and oceans. However, new research from scientists show that it is the competition between these two systems that produce the cycle of seasons and that high levels of carbon dioxide may be altering the earth's thermostat.

David Thomson, an engineer at AT&T Bell Laboratories, has discovered the onset of the seasons has shifted forward over times and in each century winter begins 1.4 days late. He thinks these changes have to do with precession, a slow, cyclic change in the orientation of Earth's Axis that resembles the wobble of a spinning top. Because of precession, in 13,000 years the Northern Hemisphere will experience summer in January and winter in June. As a result, the timing of the seasons changes slightly each year.

Thomson noted that statistics, dating from 1940, began to shift much more rapidly than precession alone could explain. He then began to compare the temperature pattern to carbon dioxide emissions and found his answer. Carbon dioxide, which traps heat in the atmosphere, was also delaying the onset of winter in the Northern Hemisphere.

The heat from radiation in the Northern Hemisphere, peaks on the summer solstice, June 22. Peak heating, for radiation and heat transport, for the entire planet is on January 3. The excess carbon dioxide is disturbing the balance between these two heating processes and affecting the seasons. In the Northern Hemisphere, because heat radiation and heat transport, peak six months apart, it's climate is influenced more by direct radiation, forcing a delayed winter. In the Southern Hemisphere, these two heating systems peak at the same time, so their seasons hardly alter. [13]

CHAPTER NINE

CANADA / THE METAPHOR

There is plenty for all! There is always enough! The universal substance is indeed abundant!

These are the words of Hilarion for Canada, and contain the metaphor of abundance and prosperity for her peoples. Canada represents the great crown of the flame for the lands sponsored by Saint Germain; it's glory graced with co-creation, abundant fields and seas, and New Age cities filled with art and music. However, it is a land where great change must take place in order to fulfill its prophecy of abundance. Again, the heart of the people is addressed and it is a heart that must soften to accept the glory of universal law.

The land is said to be held by an eagle's talons, but once this eagle loosens its grip, the dove's breast emerges, revealing a purity and innocence that feeds the entire Americas.

The earthquake is an awakening call to the people of Canada.

The jagged coastline and high cliffs represent the dangers of materialism and the difference that exists between the physical and spiritual realities.

The warming and thawing of the Canadian northlands represents the opening heart and receptivity to spiritual law.

The formation of new and abundant seas represents the manifestation and precipitation of the law of abundance.

The draining of lakes represents letting go of old ways and habits that do not serve the greater good; the widening St. Lawrence represents the opening of this country to a softer and gentler creation.

Harshness and coldness shown in this land represents areas that can be balanced through acceptance of the natural femininity metaphored in the dove's breast. It is a breast that gives with great love and tenderness; genuine sincerity and caring for creation.

Canada's destiny lies in its ability to open the playful child in life. It is seen by the Masters as a great playground of co-creation, filled with the light of joy and the sound of harmonies in music and song. Earth needs such heavenly places, where creation is recreated and rejoiced.

♥ METAPHORICALLY SPEAKING...

THE ANCIENT ART OF METAPHOR

Hermes, who is said to be the father of the arts, was known by both the Ancient Egyptians, through the Book of Thoth, and the Greeks as 'Herm', a form of Chiram. Hermes was also worshipped by the Scandinavians under the name of Odin, the Teutons as Wotan, and by some Orientals as Buddha. His ancient teachings were passed among the cultures through symbols and metaphors, which seemed to cross language barriers. Here is a brief table:

Name or Symbol	Metaphoric Meaning
Hermes	Universal Wisdom
Typhon, The Dragon	Ignorance and perversion
Dog	Intelligence and devotion
Uraeus, Symbol Of Scorpio	Regeneration
Scarab	Spiritual light
The number 3	Regeneration of the body Illumination of the mind Transmutation of the emotions
Flock of sheep	Humanity
Supreme father	Shepherd
Shepherd's Crook	Virtue guides destiny
Hammer	The Word

M ankind has held a dream and vision for the promised lands of 'milk and honey'; a home where abundance is natural and daily labors are minimal, leaving time for inspiring and uplifting endeavors of artistic expression.

This vision is the mystic message for Canada. It is also a message assured for the whole planet, when in our hearts we become again as little children and learn to play.

In the times of changes, we are asked to touch into our hearts. Only there, will we find answers to troubling questions and solutions to unanswerable problems. Sanat Kumara states this as a simple remembrance and a simple forgiveness of self. "When one enters into forgiveness, they realize the perfection of their heart. This perfection duplicates, and the radiance of this awakening extends to their brothers and sisters."

Canada's mystic message is also found in the word brotherhood, and this concept is interwoven throughout the prophecies. In example: Thirteen islands represent thirteen new starseeds or races of human beings to incarnate during the millennium. The Cooperation Mountains are said to, "bridge the world of divine form," and Canada will be known as the Bridge Of Brotherhood.

The prophecy closes as accepting perfection for all who live in the Americas and a great earth monument, Plateau Of The Rising Sun, is formed. Here, it is said the violet flame of forgiveness will be everpresent on earth and all will celebrate, "The Light of God That Never Fails."

Great source of creation.
Empower my being,
my brother,
my sister,
and my planet
with perfection
As we collectively awaken as one cell.

6. **PASHACINO**
Bridge Of Brotherhood For
All Peoples
Soltec
Canada: Alberta, British Columbia
Green Ray

7. **EABRA**
Joy; Balance; Equality
Portia
Canada: Yukon, Northwest Territories
Violet Ray

8. **JEAFRAY**
Stillness; Celebration Of The
Violet Flame
Archangel Zadkiel Of The
Seventh Ray
Amethyst
Canada: Quebec
Violet Ray

9. **UVERNO**
The Song Of God
Paul The Venetian
Canada: Manitoba, Ontario
Pink Ray

10. **YUTHOR**
Abundance Of Choice
Hilarion
Greenland
Green Ray

▲ *MYSTICALLY SPEAKING...*

THE SPARK OF CREATION IS GIVEN LIFE THROUGH INDIVIDUAL RESPONSIBILITY

"Perverted thought, uncurbed emotions and destructive actions - slay the spirit of life in man and bring down the Temple of Creation in ruins about their own heads. Illumined and sanctified for his labor by the realization of individual responsibility, the candidate goes forth to master his own lower nature - the beast that must ever stand between him and the altar of his God. The lessons of self-mastery were taught in all the Mystery Schools."
-Manly Hall

CHAPTER ELEVEN

THE GREENING MAP
JAPAN, AUSTRALIA, CHINA, INDIA, ASIA
A LITERAL INTERPETATION

The prophecy of earth changes for Asia is part of the Greening Map and the sponsor of these lands is Beloved Kuan Yin. The Greening Map is known as an area of resurrection and rebirth and the earth changes in this area reflect this theme as new lands are birthed in the millennium.

The first event for the Greening Lands is within 5 years of the activation of the ring of fire, an earthquake strikes Japan and in less than four hours Tokyo, Kawasaki and Yokohama are covered by huge tidal waves leaving the new eastern coastline of this island as far west as Maebashi. During the next three months Japan is engulfed in volcanic ash and continuous earthquake and aftershock activity.

The aftermath is shocking, and Japan now remains as three small islands. The lower, southern end of Honshu is submerged under ocean waters. Gone are the cities Osaka, Kyoto, Kobe, Okayama, Fukuyama and Hiroshima. The island of Shikoku remains, surprisingly un- scathed and thousands of survivors seek refuge in the cities of Tokushima, Matsuyama and Kochi. The western coastline of the island Kyushu is also gone, with about two-thirds of the island remains intact, however the volcanic activity is so intense, much of the remaining lands are uninhabitable. In the next 20 years the cities of Kumamoto, Kagoshima and Miyazaki are rebuilt and repopulated.

The northern portion of the larger island of Honshu remains, however its western coastline is covered by the waters of the Sea Of Japan, (known now as the Sea Of Great Mercy). The shape of this new island starts at the northern city of Aomari, extends south to the cities of Tsuruoka, Nagaoka and Fukui. The cities of Akita, Niigata, Toyama and Kanazawa are under the ocean waters. The new southern coastline wraps around the hills and mountains to Toyota and Shizuoka; then onward to Maebahi, and northern to Sendai.

The island of Hokkaido is devastated by earthquake and volcanic activity, broken into four small islands, destroying the cities of Hakodate, Sapporo and Asahikawa. By the year 2,100, a major tectonic movement raises the Sea Of Okhotsk and the new lands involve the remaining northern portion of Hokkaido including the Kitami Sanchi Mountains.

This major movement signifies the end of earth changes for the Greening Map and the rebirth of its people. New lands enlarge the island of Kyushu, forming a peninsula to the smaller islands of Tanega-Shima and Yaku-Shima. This major earth movement births a beautiful, new mountain for the peoples of Japan on Shikoku. Known as Mount Compassion, for gracing Japan with bountiful new lands, she rises to 7,000 feet. As another earth monument to the new age of peace and grace, Mt. Compassion is surrounded by new lands which now extend Shikoku's southeast corner to 32° latitude and the 134° longitude.

AUSTRALIA

Seven years after the activation of the ring of fire and two years after the sinking of Tokyo, the result of global warming and torrential rains engulf Australia. With the first shift of the poles, tectonic plates move aggressively and the continent opens, revealing an underwater ocean and the Blissful Sea is born. This large sea's northern mouth begins at Cape York Peninsula, travels eastern through Queensland, extending down through New South Wales; Broken Hill becomes its beachfront city, with the southern mouth opening into the Southern Ocean. The formation of this great sea destroys the cities of Elizabeth and Adelaide. Its western boundaries include the Northern Territory and South Australia; buffering up to the Macdonnell Mountains, with Alice Springs and Mount Isa becoming prosperous seaports in the new age.

The next great shift of lands in the Greening Map, finds the northern and western coastlines of Australia slipping into the Indian Ocean. The northern city of Darwin is engulfed by the ocean waters in this event and more waters lap the edge of the city of Perth. From

Melville Island to West Cape Howe, the coastline is significantly changed, with much erosion and unstable lands for a 20 year period.

In the year 2,100, the raising of the Sea Of Okhotsk heralds the completion of the Greening Map, and a massive land ridge, Protection Bluff, raises off the great barrier reef in Australia's northeast corner. A southern bay is birthed, as lands sink in this great earth movement. This new inlet, Bay Of Mystery, engulfs the Great Victoria Desert, halting at the Musgrave Range.

Much of the eastern coastline of Australia and New South Wales, remains unscathed during the times of earth change, and many of the population moves to these areas. However, several of its cities experience change through shifting coastlines and raising waters. Melbourne is abandoned for 100 years and rebuilt to flourish again in the new age.

The final earth change event for Australia is the southeast pivoting of Tasmania Island in the year 2158.

ASIA / CHINA

Two years after the sinking of Tokyo, mainland Asia is struck by an explosive earthquake, shattering her lands and creating many new bays and inlets filled with ocean waters. The first bay formed is Regeneration Bay, with her waters forming a huge sea cradled by the Greater Khaigan Mountains. The newly created seaport cities of this great earth change are: Kamsomolsk, Shenyang, Shijiazhuang, Huang, Nanyang, and the bay forms an inlet to the city of Nanchang. The city of Hangzhou becomes an open port city to Regeneration Bay and The Sea Of Mercy.

The Three Heavenly Islands remain between Regeneration Bay and The Sea Of Mercy. The Sikhote Aln Mountains form the first large island to the north; the second Heavenly Island is the remaining lands of North Korea on the Chinese border. The third island is the remaining land of South Korea. These cities are covered by ocean waters: Khabarovsi, Qiqihar, Harbin, Jilin, Changchun, Baicheng, Fushun, Anshan, Beijing, Dalian, Qingdao, Seoul, Pyangyang and Vladivostok. The loss of life is extremely heavy in this area.

As the waters of the East China Sea rise, (now called the Sea Of Mercy), many other Chinese cities are also lost: Wuxi, Shanghai, Wenzhou and Fuzhou.

Throughout the times of changes the Island of Taiwan, the Philippines, and the Indonesian and Malaysian islands are very unstable geophysically. Activated volcanoes erupt continuously and torrential rains erode their lands. Many of their peoples leave before these lands disappear into the Pacific Ocean with the rising of the Sea Of Okhotsk.

Great shifts in the Himalayan mountains activate the next earth movement which change the face of Asia again. Forming the Rim Of Eternal Balance and The Blazing Bay, sinking and rising lands destroy Vietnam, Thailand, Laos, Cambodia and most of Burma. The Blazing Bay creates new seaport cities for interior China: Lanzhou and Xining; the western coast of this bay is cradled by the Imaglha Mountains and is very steep and rocky with high cliffs over 2,000 feet high. Cities lost in this earth change: Chengdu, Neijiang, Chongqing, Zunyi, Hanoi and Hong Kong.

Through the massive global warming, much of northern Asia is eroded and washed away and a new massive body of water, the Ocean Of Balance is formed. By the year 2,200, several larger islands remain, now named the Bounty Islands. The weather becomes much warmer in this area supporting bountiful and fruitful farms. A large fresh water lake is formed in new north Asia, near the Yablonovoy Mountains, called the Lake Of Deep Truth. To the south of this great lake, lies Mongolia and the Gobi Desert, her lands restored to a rich, abundant state. This area is now called the Fertile Plain, and waters from newly formed fresh water lakes are used to irrigate her many crops.

In the year 2,100, the final earth change event is signaled for the Greening Lands with the rising of the Sea Of Okhotsk. This rising starts with major shifts of the Japan trench and large mountains appear north of Sapporo, Japan. This signals more great mountains birthed from movements of the Kuril Trench and the Okhotsk Basin. By the year 2,660, much of this great sea has evaporated, leaving one of the largest earth change monuments on the planet. Named the Land Of Light, this new plateau is surrounded by a large sea to the north called the Sea Of Clarity.

INDIA / PAKISTAN / SOUTHWEST ASIA

During the times of the great rains, the Ganges River swells over seven times its size and much of India is pelted by typhoon storms. During the great deluge of monsoon activity, a large river runs throughout the middle of India named the River Of 7 Waters. Heavy winds and erosive rains break apart the eastern coastline, leaving India a swampy marsh. But it is not until the great earth shift in the Himalayan Mountains, (which rise to even greater heights and re-named the Awakening Mountains), that India's face is changed for the new age.

In this earthquake, the swampy Ganges river basin sinks, opening the eastern side of India all the way to New Delhi. Within the next two years, another earthquake strikes and another bay is formed on the western side of India, again opening the ocean bay this time to Delhi and cutting a swath through the eastern half of Pakistan. India now hangs onto Asia connected by a narrow isthmus of land, approximately 150 miles wide. Within 750 to 1000 years this isthmus erodes, and India becomes one of the largest islands of the earth.

The new eastern bay, called the Sea of Calm, creates seaport cities of New Delhi, Kanpur and Girago in Nepal. Cities destroyed in this earth change are Calcutta, Haora, Bengal, Chiti Gong, Dhaka, Bhagalpur, Patna, Varanasi, Allahabad, Kanpur, Lucknow, and Agra.

The western bay, named Serenity Bay, creates seaport cities of Delhi; extends north to Lahore and Islambad, Pakistan; and the southern Pakistan city of Sukkur. Cities in India destroyed in this earth change activity are Bhavnnjar, Vadodora, Ahmadabad, Jodhpur, Bikaner. Cities in Pakistan destroyed in this earth change activity are Karachi, Hydesabad, Sellwan, Banawalpur and Multan. The southern coastline of Pakistan is flooded, and the city of Jwadar is under water.

With these major earth movements, the entire coastline of India sinks approximately 25 to 50 miles inland. Susceptible western cities are: Suras, Bombay, Pune, Kolhapur, Mangalone, Madurai. The flooding of the Godavari river opens another small bay on the eastern coast and the city of Warangal becomes a seaport to the Bay Of Bengal, renamed the Bay Of Scented Flowers. Another small bay opens on the northeastern coastline of India near the Sea Of Calm, creating the seaport city of Jamsheds. Succeptable eastern cities are: Puri,

Vizianagaran, Vijayawada, Nellore, Madras, Pondicherry, and Negapattinam.

The island of Sri Lanka, renamed the Holy Island, is reduced to one half of it's size by the raising oceans and one city remains; Kandy. In the year 2100, new lands rise off of its northern coast.

Other earth change events for this area include the birth of thousands of tiny islands as the Carlsberg Ridge and Chagos Laccadive Plateau rise off the coast of India in the Arabian Sea and Indian Ocean, (renamed the Glory Ocean). These islands begin to appear in the year 2050 and are named the Shimmering Islands.

☞ LITERALLY SPEAKING...

THE BENEFITS OF VOLCANIC ASH

Bentonite, or volcanic ash, has incredible detoxifying powers.

"The ability of volcanic ash to do this stems from the great electro-positive potential in the ash as a result of its fiery, (yang), origin." Volcanoes are the safety valves of the planet and their simultaneous explosion could cleanse the toxicity levels of the planet, primarily radioactivity. "This is not the end of the world, but that very massage needed to keep the world from ending." [14]

CHAPTER TWELVE

THE GREENING MAP
JAPAN, AUSTRALIA, CHINA, INDIA, ASIA
THE METAPHOR

T he changing heart of the lands of Asia and India, again, are metaphored in its name, the Greening Map. These are the people called to rebirth and resurrect universal thought to lead the largest mass of earth's people into a life that grows from the heart. These are lands to be filled with life's vigor and life's great presence!

Throughout the literal interpretation of the prophecies for these lands, one cannot help but be touched with waves of sadness. Over one billion lives could be lost in such a series of geophysical earth changes. The paradox of this message, is that those who have so much to lose, also have the most to gain. When seen, not as a message of loss, but, as a message to use wisdom, instead of suffering and wars, society gains the priceless spiritual gifts of forgiveness, mercy and compassion.

It is a message for all of us. It is a call to the unity and oneness for all life...the presence of life, and our duty to preserve life in all of its forms. Here lies the planet's future and destiny with this simple and powerful metaphor. To value life, first, we must honor it.

The time has come that we must awaken the laws of ecological alchemy. Here, the people are called to honor the tree of life; its leaves, stems, branches and roots.

According to the prophecy, the land responds instantly. Assimilating the natural law of life, abundant agricultural plains form in Asian wasteland. It is said that India will be filled with so many types of new flowers that the sea around her will carry their fragrance. The fragrance of life and goodness is prophesied for these lands, and this goodness and simplicity comes from an understanding of mercy and compassion for all of life.

The four hour tidal waves of destruction symbolize that the great need is now. Now, is the time for hearts in these lands to awaken and hear the prophecy with all senses.

Erupting volcanoes symbolize the end of conflict and self-righteousness. A time has come for a peaceful surrender to happiness, bliss and eternal life.

Disappearing cities represents the cold and invisible heart. These are people who are called to find life again and rejoice in the oneness of all existence and creation.

The rising of new lands represents that faith, charity and hope restores and renews hearts with gratitude. The new lands rising in these areas represent that within all of humanity is a deep, fruitful desire to restore and renew ourselves when we get off balance. The process of restoration is a blessing; it's renewing cycles prepare us for a deeper and more meaningful co-creation.

Torrential rains represent the cries of humanity, asking for reprieve and correct rightness with life. Here lies the need to accept responsibility in order to understand inherent divinity and co-creatorship.

Lands engulfed by waters shows a great mouth, (ocean waters), opening and swallowing; hence the paradox that life preys upon life. Gulping and gorging movements indicate a spiritual starvation and the deep need to restore the god-man in a continuous, consistent manner. Here is a call for balance, and enactment of the mystic law that life begats life. The eye of God opens. The rising of Mt. Compassion symbolizes the gift of clarity and all seeing balance.

New bays and seas show the openness and innocence of awakening and opening to the divine will and plan. Here, the teachers of compassion and mercy guide each student to rejoice in the oneness of all life.

The pivoting of Tasmania shows that a new direction is now taken upon the planet. This new course of compassion, restores our hearts and vision for a new age.

The rising of the Shimmering Islands shows that the compassionate heart shines clearly; its light is visible and usable for all conditions.

CHAPTER THIRTEEN

THE GREENING MAP
JAPAN, AUSTRALIA, CHINA, INDIA, ASIA
THE MYSTIC & COSMIC MESSAGE

The message for humanity with the prophecy of The Greening Map again is simple; it is the message of oneness for all expression of life. Its mystic application lies in its universal experience with compassion and mercy, and our willingness to rise above the perception of sorrow and suffering to find its healing power. It is this mystic oneness that restores and resurrects the human plan to a heavenly plan, filled with the lush treasures of divinity.

The Greening Lands, map a heavenly plan of universal rhythm and harmony of divine co-creation, as five of the Archangels sponsor golden cities for the millennium. This indicates a great focus of heavenly service in these lands and the great golden city of Gobi is again opened to serve humanity.

Many of the avatars and great teachers of humanity reappear to serve this great age of grace: Lord Himalaya, Lord Meru, and Lord Guatama. Great Divine Mother, (who represents the mother planet), makes a mighty appearance and sponsors the city of Kantan with Archangel Raphael.

New lands appear above the continent of Australia, and are named the Lands Of Oneness in celebration to the Law of All. Here, the peoples of the Greening Lands merge into collective oneness with life and the world. It is this joining and unity that is expressed in her seventeen wondrous golden cities.

I call forth the cellular awakening.
Let wisdom, love and power stream forth to this cell,
This cell that we all share.

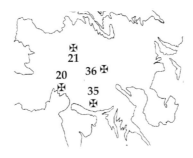

20. **ADJATAL**
Awakening!
Lord Himalaya
Asia Minor: Pakistan (Jammu), Afghanistan, Northern India (Kashmir), Russia (Pamir), China.
Blue & Gold Ray

21. **PURENSK**
The Great Gift Of Love, Wisdom & Power
Faith, Hope, Charity
Russia: Kirgizskaja, Kazachskaja. China: Xinjiang Uygur Zizhiqu
Blue, Yellow & Pink Rays

35. **ZASKAR**
Simplicity
Reya
China: Tibet, Xizang Zizhiqu
White Ray

36. **GOBI**
City Of Balance
Lord Meru
Archangel Uriel Of The Sixth Ray
China: Over the Qilian Shan Mountains
next to the Gobi Desert.
Ruby & Gold Ray

22. **PRANA**
The Continuous Heart; Adoration
Archangel Chamuel Of The Third Ray
Central India
Pink Ray

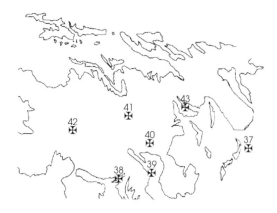

37. ARCTURA

Freedom / Precipitation / Rhythm Of Universal Harmony
Arcturus, Elohim Of The Seventh Ray
Diana
China: Sichuan Szechwan, Yuanan
Violet Ray

38. NOMAKING

Wisdom / Illumination
Power Of Attention / Perception
Cassiopeia, Elohim of Wisdom
Minverva, Goddess of Wisdom
China: Nei Mongol Aiahiqu,
Shaanxi Shengi, Shanxi Shangi.
Yellow Ray

39. PRESCHING

City For The Angels / Love Of Ordered Service
Archangel Jophiel Of The Second Ray
China: Jilikirin (Manchuria);
North Korea
Yellow Ray

40. KANTAN

Regeneration / Assimilation Dedication
Great Divine Mother
Archangel Raphael Of The Fifth Ray
Russia: Rossijskaja. China: Nei
Monggol Zizhiqu (Manchuria)
Green Ray

41. HUE

City Of Many Paths / Earnestness
Lord Guatama, The First of The Zarathustras
Russia: Siberia (Apex is located
at Gora Kamen).
Violet Ray

42. SIRCALWE

Circle Of Life
Group Of Twelve
Served by an everpresent and
everchanging group of twelve known
as the Brotherhood & Sisterhood
of Light.
Russia: East Siberia, cradled by the
Verchojanskji Chrebet & Chrebet
Cerskogo Mountains.
White Ray

43. ARKANA

Transfiguration / Ascension
Archangel Gabriel Of The Fourth Ray
Russia: East Siberia, the Arctic Circle
runs through the apex. Surrounded by
the An Ujsku Chrebet and Penzinskij
Chrebet Mountains.
White Ray

46. GREIN
Consecration / Service To The Upliftment Of Humanity
Through Scientific Development
Viseria, (Divine Compliment To Soltec)
New Zealand: South Island, this Golden City Vortex will
serve the southern part of New Lemuria.
Green Ray

47. CLAYJE
City Of Many Planets / Universal Oneness
Orion, Elohim Of Divine Love
Australia: Tasmania, covers the entire island.
Pink Ray

48. ANGELICA
Twin City To Clayje; City Of Divine Love
Angelica, (Twin Ray of The Elohim
of Divine Love, Orion)
Australia: Queensland
Pink Ray

49. SHEAHAH
Purity / Transmutation
Astrea, (Twin Ray of The Elohim Of Purity, Claire)
Australia: Northern Territory, Uluru National Park.
White Ray

50. FRON
Focus / Aligns To The First Golden City, Gobean
Desiree
Australia: Western Australia, apex near Lake Ballard.
Blue Ray

▲ MYSTICALLY SPEAKING...

THIS IS A TIME FOR US TO ACCEPT CHANGE
The earth changes are an opportunity for us to explore the idea of change
and evolve spiritually. We must change ourselves enough that this change
reflects in our societies, governments and environments. We have a
conscious choice in the upcoming earth changes and that choice will help
determine the outcome.
"Change is the Law! All change manifest spirally. All things decay or
degenerate from within. Civilizations as well as substantial things."
                                                           -Jerry Canty

★★★★★★★★★★★★★★★★★★

CHAPTER FOURTEEN

THE MAP OF EXCHANGES
EUROPE, AFRICA, MIDDLE EAST, WESTERN ASIA
A LITERAL INTERPRETATION

This earth change prophecy for Europe and Africa, is perhaps the most alarming of all prophecies. As the earth changes close in the islands of Japan, Europe chimes in with riddling earthquakes and volcanic explosions, thus the dawn of the new world is near.

It is here in the prophecies that the last vestige of miscreation is removed and the mythical 'torn curtain' is lifted as too, is the perception of separation. As the earth accepts fourth dimensional consciousness, alignment shifts the layers of the atmosphere and great tears occur in the first three layers of the atmosphere. The phenomenon of ice sheeting occurs, as huge layers of ice, (approximately one mile thick), drop on areas throughout Europe and Western Asia, on areas ten square miles in diameter.

Thus, Europe and Africa become areas of exchange, where the bridging of conscious collective thought extends its creative wave onward to the cosmos. Through this expansion and assimilation, the earth and its people receive great rays of universal healing. Here, two of the most focused Ascended Masters of healing step into sponsorship: Beloved Nada for Europe and Beloved Kuthumi for Africa.

The first event for Europe is prophesied to begin around the year 2,000. After the sinking of the upper portion of Vancouver Island, (Canada), tectonic plates in the Atlantic ocean move, and a series of earthquakes strike northern Europe. Especially effected are Norway, Sweden, Finland and Eastern Europe, with this earth movement felt as far east into Moscow. Soon, torrential rains hit the coast of England, France and Spain and with the second shift of the pole, lands in England, France and Germany are engulfed by the newly formed

Ocean of Balance. Cities engulfed in this earth change are: Helsinki, Stockholm, Oslo, Copenhagen, London, Dublin, Hamburg, Berlin, Warsaw, Krakow, Ladz, Amsterdam, Brussels, Paris, and Bordeaux. Global warming brings shifting ice and glaciers. Combined with raising waters and erosion; the breakup of the lands forms many new islands in upper Ukraine, Sweden, Germany and France. These cities become new age seaports for the Ocean Of Balance: Glasgow, Sherffield, Manchester, Essen, Prague, Berdichev and Galati.

The lands of Iceland raise, with the Reykjanes Ridge raising in a tail-like shape on the southwestern portion of the island.

Tears in the ozone layer brings great sheets of ice crashing onto eastern Europe and remaining parts of Poland and Germany. This occurs for approximately 6 to 9 months. The next event for the Map of Exchanges is the formation of the Sea Of Grace. This corresponds to the raising of the Himalayan Mountains into the Awakening Mountains around the year 2,028. As this massive earth change occurs, The Black Sea, Azov Sea, Caspian Sea and Aral Sea form one great body of water, The Sea of Grace. Lands lost in this earth change are: sections of northern Turkey, parts of Iran and Afghanistan, the Ukraine, eastern coastlines of Romania and Bulgaria, and extending north to the Ural Mountains. Newly created seaport cities are: Zonguldak, Tehran (approximately 100 miles from the new coastline), Samarkan, Turkestam, Baykanur, Turgay. The Ural mountains form a large island, called The Shiny Pearl. This island becomes a great trade center for the Ocean Of Balance with seaport cities covering her coastline. Several of these present day cities are: Kuybyshev, Ocenburg, Aktyu, Aktyubinsk, and Sterlitamak. During the earth changes many people will migrate to this island and it evolves into one of the most prosperous lands in the new age.

At the close of the period of cataclysmic earth changes for the world, many scientific experiments evolve into a major nuclear detonation to save southern Europe. However, through this man-made change, (which enlarges the Mediterranean and Red Seas), The Sea Of Eternal Change is born. Her waters cover the lands of: Libya, Egypt, Sudan, Israel, Jordan, western Syria, the western coastline of Saudi Arabia, northern Ethiopia, and Tunisia. Much of Italy, Yugoslavia, Albania, all of Greece and southern Turkey are covered by ocean waters. Cities lost in this change are: Rome, Venice, Naples, Barj, Tirane, Athens, Izmir, Thessaloniki, Tripoli, Tunis, Benghazi, Alexandria, Cairo, Yafo, Beirut, Tel Aviv and Jerusalem.

New Age seaports for The Sea Of Eternal Change are: Anngba, Qacenhna, Ghat, Merawe, Omdurman, Khartoum, Kaka, Gore, Murnos, Adis Abeba, Ganden and Asmera. On the eastern coast of the Sea Of Change: Suna, Mecca, Medina, and Tobuk. More cities surrounding this new sea: Damascus, Aleppo, Kongo, Sofia, Sanaievo, Zapreb, Milan, and Turin.

Within the next 20 to 30 years, the Persian Gulf, (now named Bay Of Holy Prayer), widens through more shifting of tectonic plates, forming another large bay into the Glory (Indian) Ocean. Lands lost are the western coastlines of Oman, Saudi Arabia, and Iraq. New age coastline cities are: Riyadh and An Najaf. The Euphrates and Tigres River basin is covered with this new sea and the western coastline of Iran is buffered by the Zagros Mountains.

The final land movements for the map of exchanges begin in the year 2,100 as new lands enlarge the countries of Portugal and Spain. Lands enlarge the southern tip of Africa and the countries of Namibia and South Africa and the Island of Madagascar doubles in size. With this movement, the western coastline of Africa falls into the Atlantic Ocean, creating new coastlines in the countries of Algeria, Morocco, submerging all of Western Sahara, Mauritania and Senegal. A new coastal bay, Bay Of Protection, enlarges the Gulf Of Guinea cutting into central Africa's Nigeria and Cameroon. Central African Republic and the country of Chad now enjoy access to the Atlantic Ocean.

The southern coastlines of the African countries of Guinea, Ivory Coast and Ghana drop into the Atlantic Ocean / Guinea Basin. The countries of Sierra Leone and Liberia are submerged in this earth change as well as most of Togo. Gone are the cities of Freetown, Monrovia, Abidjan, Accra, Lome, Porto Novo, Lagos, and Bioka. A four hundred mile swath cuts into the western coast of southern Congo and Angola, sinking all of Cabinda.

The eastern coastline of Africa breaks into a series of tiny islands, creating a large coastal bay near Lake Victoria and the Rift Valley. This earth change destroys all of Somalia and Ethiopia becomes a seaport country to Glory Ocean. Kenya, Tanzania and Zimbabwe also grace

Glory's waters, and Mozambique is broken into many small islands. South Africa splits apart and the inland country of Botswana becomes a seaport country. Cities gone in this earth change event are: Muqdisho, Dar es Salaam, Maputo and Durban.

Throughout the years 2,100 to 2,200 major earth changes complete for the existing world's lands, however, during this time, new lands emerge on the earth's face. The rising of the ancient lands of Lemuria complete the earth's entry into the millennium of peace and grace. The first new lands of Lemuria are seen northwest of the Hawaiian Islands, around the 30° latitude and 170° longitude. Another large continent reveals itself enlarging the lands of New Zealand from approximately the 55° latitude northern to the 5° latitude. This new continent, larger than Australia, also includes the Fiji and Somoan Islands. The birth of this new land sees the raising of the Tonga and Kermadec Ridge and the Austral Seamount Chain.

As the ice caps melt in global warming, new lands are revealed at the South Pole. The final earth movement comes to the planet around the year 2,457 with new lands forming a peninsula on the south pole region with the raising of the Scotia Ridge.

☞ LITERALLY SPEAKING...

THE LAW OF UNIFORMITY

The social backdrop of war torn Europe, not laboratory research, set a climate that developed the scientific theory, the Law Of Uniformity. After 25 years of revolution and war, 18th century Europeans sought harmony in all things, and developed convincing dialects that reflected their desire for peace. The Law Of Uniformity, would leave a mark upon science that would remain unchallenged for over 100 years. It is based on the idea that the geology of our planet formed within the perimeters of natural law, taking extremely long periods of time to mature and that nothing extreme or chaotic could ever occur in nature. The theory was elevated to it's position by a young attorney, Charles Lyell, around 1830. Lyell sought to devoid any theory of extraterrestial, (asteroids, meteors, etc.), interaction with the earth, and temporarily closed the scientific mind to theories based upon cataclysmic geology. Lyell's use of the Law Of Uniformity painted a world aimed towards a rigid order in nature that evolved all things, inspiring one of his more famous students, Charles Darwin.

CHAPTER FIFTEEN

THE MAP OF EXCHANGES
EUROPE, AFRICA, MIDDLE EAST, WESTERN ASIA
THE METAPHOR

The metaphor for change in these lands lies in the phrase, "as above, so below." In the physical body, the heart, is also known as the center of exchange and its condition often determines overall health. This is clearly where the overall outcome for our transitional shift in expanding consciousness will be determined and the anchoring of heaven on earth begins.

The earth changes in these lands is drastic, the heavens opening and literally pouring upon the lands. Here, the people are asked to open their hearts and let blessings of creation pour into them. The definition of exchange means to give and receive reciprocally. The challenge reflected in the prophecy for the peoples of these lands is that a time has come to give first, or metaphorically to open up, and then receive.

This is a heart that exchanges, openly and willingly. It is also a heart that opens the doorway for the whole world to receive heaven.

The dropping of the ice sheets signifies that heaven is now and it is time to correct our thinking.

Earthquakes and torrential rains metaphor the need to restore clear vision and repeat the message that we are all equal co-creators.

The raising lands of Iceland represent the father, (heavenly), energies anchoring themselves onto the mother planet for its new journey in co-creation.

The sinking of lands in the Map Of Exchanges represents the need to give silence and 'rest' to the old ways and habits of doing things. "The earth is old and tired," defines the prophecy best and clearly here.

It is time to walk gently with her, in service and co-creation; honoring her peaceful passage which designs and shapes a New World.

The Sea Of Grace, represents that the law of heaven is restored to the planet and father and mother unite again in a joyful conception of god-man.

The raising of the lands in Europe represents humanity's application of spiritual principles through simple truth: Equality for all life.

The forming of the Sea Of Eternal Change represents the need to recognize universal laws of creation. It is this earth change metaphor that shows the value of one person's actions, actually chooses that same action for many other people.

The rising of New Lemuria represents the restoration of earth as our true home and paradise. Recognizing the value of 'growing where we are planted', our fall from grace is relatively short lived and each day is a new creation in the infinite garden. Here, we are reminded to be happy and joyful in paradise and that freedom and happiness is created through our choices.

❤ METAPHORICALLY SPEAKING...

MATHEMATICAL METAPHORS OF HARMONY

"The thinking of consciousness, the thinking you and I know by direct experience, is without restraint. We are free to think as we wish, and all our thoughts are equally real and productive of the conditions of our experience. But some thoughts harmonize with each other, and others are antagonistic to each other. The best illustration is the numerical symbolism called mathematics. $2 \times 2 = 4$ is indicative of concepts that harmonize with each other. $2 \times 2 = 3$ is indicative of concepts that are inharmonious. Both are equally real as concepts, but one indicates an absolute harmony, and the other an inharmony.

The descriptive term for those thoughts that harmonize with each other is oneness or unity. The oneness or unity of mathematics is called its principle. And, the oneness or unity of our thinking can be called its principle. Religion, responding to an intuitive recognition of the possibility of oneness or unity in our thinking, has derived from it what it terms God or the Deity."

-Bob Welb, Consciousness Network
Seattle, Washington

CHAPTER SIXTEEN

THE MAP OF EXCHANGES
EUROPE, AFRICA, MIDDLE EAST, WESTERN ASIA
THE MYSTIC & COSMIC MESSAGE

The mystic message for the planet in these final earth changes prophecies is the simplest and by far the most profound. Here, we are asked to anchor heaven on earth and to do so we must open our hearts and freely choose it to be so. Here is the return to the law inside oneself and the emergence of a new conscience. This conscience is based on the logic of the unity of all things beginning with conscious actions and an understanding of their purpose and cosmic meaning. We are asked to not only accept spiritual law, but to fulfill it.

"So be it!", Babaji says when commanding a fruitful desire into action. Here lies the mysticism in self-mastery through a life unfolding from the "world of the wondrous." This is the evolving victory for humanity, as the fourth dimension transits across the earth. Freedom is no longer a thought or feeling, but an infinite union. The hope for our new beginning is placed in the center of our independent attainment of inner unity and harmony. Here, we unite in our heart with all things and allow a cosmic consciousness to rule co-creation. A peaceable kingdom comes and ...SO BE IT!, each day as we choose and receive through our choice.

Great spark of creation awaken the Divine Plan Of Perfection.
So we may share the one perfected cell,
I AM.

The seventeen golden cities for the Map of Exchanges are:

11. **STIENTA**
    Inner Vision
    Archangel Michael Of The First Ray
    Iceland
    Blue Ray

12. **DENASHA**
    Divine Justice For Humanity
    Nada
    United Kingdom: Scotland
    Yellow Ray

13. **AMERIGO**
    God In All
    Godfre
    Europe: Spain
    Gold Ray

14. **GRUECHA**
    Strength In Truth
    Hercules
    Europe: Norway, Sweden, Denmark
    Blue Ray

15. **BRAUN**
    Glory; Achievement
    Victory
    Europe: Germany, Poland,
    Czechoslovakia
    Yellow Ray

16. **AFROM**
    Purity / Ascension
    Se Ray, (Twin Ray of Serapis Bey)
    Claire, Elohim Of Purity
    Europe: Hungary, Romania. Russia:
    Moldavia, Ukrainskaja
    White Ray

17. **GANAKRA**
    The All Seeing City; Divine Focus;
    Concentration
    Vista, Elohim Of The Fifth Ray
    Asia Minor: Turkey
    Green Ray

18. MESOTAMP
Happiness
Mohammed
Asia minor: Turkey, Iraq, Iran. Russia: Arm'anskaja, Azerbajdzanskaja
Yellow Ray

19. SHEHEZ
Peaceful; Serenity; Calm
Tranquility, Elohim Of Peace
Asia minor: Iran, Afghanistan.
Russia: Turkmenskaja
Ruby & Gold Ray

23. GANDAWAN
Infinite Garden
Kuthumi
Africa: Algeria (The tropic of Cancer runs through the apex.).
Ruby & Gold Ray

24. KRESHE
Aligns To The Silent Star
A City In Service To Elemental Life!
Lord Of Nature
Amaryllis, Goddess Of Spring
Africa: Botswana, Namibia, Angola, Zambia
Ruby & Gold Ray

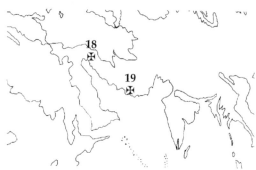

25. PEARLANU
Forgiveness
Lotus
Africa: Madagascar
Violet Ray

26. UNTE
City Of Grace & Ministration To Humanity
Donna Grace, (Twin Ray Of Archangel Uriel)
Africa: Tanzania, Kenya (The apex is Mt. Meru.).
Ruby & Gold Ray

27. LARAITO
Divine Understanding; Illumination
Lanto & Laura
Africa: Ethiopia
Yellow Ray

44. MOUSEE

The Eye Of Fire
Kona
New Lemuria: The rising of the Emperor Seamounts forms the new land for this Golden City Vortex. It now exists at approximately 36° latitude and 178° longitude. The Midway Islands are to the south.
Gold & Aquamarine Ray

45. DONJAKEY

First City Of The Golden Ray / New Lemuria
Pacifica, Elohim Of The Golden Ray
New Lemuria: Again, new lands to raise in the earth changes sponsor this Golden City Vortex. Currently in the Pacific Ocean, 179° longitude and the latitude at the apex is the Tropic of Capricorn. The Cook Islands are to the east.
Gold & Aquamarine Ray

51. CRESTA

Eternal Protection / Healing & Clarity For Mankind
Archangel Crystiel Of The Eighth Ray
Antarctica: Near Marguerite Bay, apex is located on Eternity Range.
Gold & Aquamarine Ray

CHAPTER SEVENTEEN

THE LAW OF OPPOSITES
KALI-YUGA & THE BIRTH OF A GOLDEN AGE
YOU ARE A YUGA

On the subject of earth changes two distinct opinions have developed. One, that earth changes are not necessary, and with the proper attitude and actions, devastation will be circumvented and an ensuing age of peace and prosperity for the earth and her peoples will reign. The second opinion sees the necessity of earth changes to cleanse and purify the earth and humanity's current state of self destruction. In both scenarios, balance is the desired outcome.

THE LAW OF OPPOSITES

Everything in creation is based upon the law of opposites. All things appear in twos, or, known in many spiritual traditions as *duality*. Duality is seen everywhere; literally, metaphorically and mystically. For instance: Rich/Poor. Fear/Courage. Light/Dark. The examples are endless. Even our own body is divided into male and female, the left side is female and the right, male.

Creation is visible and invisible, and all dimensions, planes, levels of awareness are subject to the law of opposites. However, it is important to understand that all manifestations are dual expressions of the *One*. This *One* is important to understand in order to comprehend how all interpretations of earth changes prophecies have their place in the motion that exists between laws of opposites. It is also important to understand while certain prophecies may oppose one another, they come together creating a balance.

Visualize this, a simple playground teeter-totter. On one side is Male, (Yang), and on the other side is Female, (Yin). The center is the fulcrum, or in this case, the One. The One is the source of the teeter-totter between Male and Female. It is the source of the interchange between the two opposing forces and always stays the same. *(See diagram)*

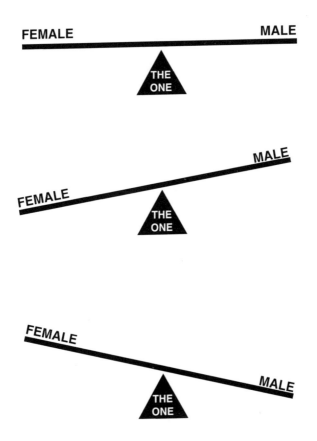

You'll note, that with each movement, Male or Female change position in the interchange of energy. One is up, or one is down. You'll also notice that in the interchange of energy, all things are forever changing into their opposites. This is a natural law and rules again, all created things. This cycle of change rules seasons and weather. It rules plants and animals, it rules the earth in its motion around the sun, and it rules you and me. This law of eternal change is also known as the law of balance.

See how the teeter-totter works? Every movement one side makes, the other side must answer, yet, there is always the changeless point. The fulcrum. The changeless. The timeless. The *One*. It is the source of the movement, and yet it never moves! Since it never changes, it is the only thing that is real! It is the point of perfect balance and contains *both* sides.

KALI-YUGA AND THE BIRTH OF A GOLDEN AGE

Man has spent ages developing systems that map the cycles of change. Many of these ancient systems measured the movement of forces based upon equinoxes and solstices. Astrology uses the movement of constellations, to calculate the influence of energy in motion, on all created things. Since all things change and move, the Ancients knew that understanding this movement would help them to understand the tendencies of the future. It's always nice to know if you're going up and it's always nice to prepare for your landing when you're going down.

The Greek mystics taught that the world would always travel through four ages: the Golden Age, the Silver Age, the Bronze Age and the Iron Age. This teaching closely resembles the four Yugas of the Hindus: Krita-Yuga, Treta-Yuga, Dvapara-Yuga and Kali-Yuga. Their calculation is based upon the twelve signs of the zodiac and is described as follows: "In each of the 12 signs, (the zodiac), there are 1800 minutes; multiply this number by 12 you have 21600; e.g. 1800 x 12 = 21600. Multiply this 21600 by 80 and it will give 1,728,000, which is the duration of the first age, called Krita Yuga. If the same number be multiplied by 60, it will give 1,296,000, the years of the second age, Treta-Yuga. The same number multiplied by 40 gives 864,000, the length of the third age, Dvapara-Yuga. The same multiplied by 20 gives 432,000, the fourth age Kali-Yuga." [15] Each of these four ages represent the cycles of duration of all things, birth, growth, maturity and decay.

The Ancients and Sages who structured these incredible systems are long gone, but the Ages and the Yugas march on, charting the patterns of motion that can still tell us alot about today and tomorrow. According to sources, we are still living out the age of Iron, a cycle of decay, the Kali-Yuga. But, there's good news. After this cycle is complete, the teeter-totter raises back up and we enter into a cycle of birth that will last over 1.5 million years. The Golden Age, Krita Yuga. I have merged these ancient teachings with Ascended Master teachings in the chart that follows. Here, you will see that the age that we are currently experiencing, is paving the pathway for an age of Gold. *(Kali-Yuga is the Iron age of industrialization ruled by money, symbolized by the suit of coins in the Tarot. According to sources, this age began in the year 3,102 B.C. Six thousand years before the end of Dvapara-Yuga, the continent of Atlantis sunk into the now Atlantic Ocean.)*

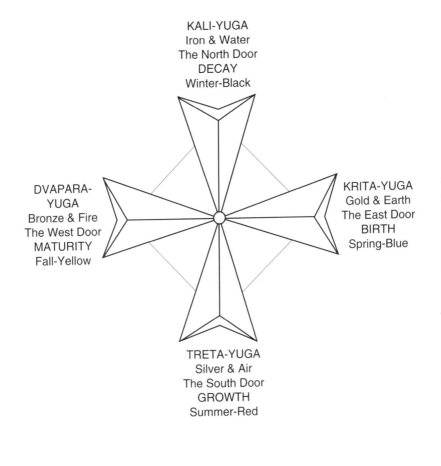

This Golden Age is ruled by the earth element and all things that live on the earth. Everything, including the earth, (Beloved Babajeran), is reborn at this time. This cycle is also ruled by the priesthood, so I'm sure during Krita-Yuga we can expect to see the rebirth of many useful and beautiful spiritual ceremonies. During Kali-Yuga, even though it is a cycle of decay, many seeds are planted that will sprout during the age of gold. *(In the tarot, Krita-Yuga is symbolized by the suit of cups.)*

YOU ARE A YUGA

It is important to remember that in any cycle, in the center of all things, is still the source, the real you. In Ascended Master teachings it is known as the *I AM*. Others call it the Higher Self, God, Source, the One. You cannot disconnect the center from the playground teeter-totter anymore than you can disconnect god from man or light from motion. In essence, this source commands the motion between any pairs of opposites, the cycles of all ages and Yugas. You are a Yuga!

We can also learn about the inseparable bond that exists between man and nature through the knowledge of the ONE, and emerge with a new and wondrous potential. Jerry Canty, in *Eternal Massage*, The George Ohsawa Macrobiotic Foundation, Inc. Publishers, 1971, page 7, lends his profound prophecies for the days to come, "Even to the degree that man's most casual thoughts affects the motion of the galaxies and that this motion affects his thoughts. Nor is this connection, 'mystical or undefinable.' It is dynamically verifiable. The unified science of the Millennium must rest on this verification, and man will know his true unity with all things unto the One."

Some day we won't just believe, accept or understand; through experience, we'll *know*.

SPIRITUAL INSIGHTS ON
EARTH CHANGES TO CONSIDER

1.   Since the planet and the human share the same composition we are virtually one. You cannot disconnect the two.

2.   Our world is a thought and feeling hologram created from the many kingdoms, (mineral, vegetable, animal, human, etc.), that inhabit it. The earth is a system. Our body is a system. These systems are interrelated.

3.   Every individual thought, desire and action is recorded and subsequently influences and creates the collective consciousness.

4.   Collective Consciousness plays a major role in the outcome of events. It can make the difference between a cataclysmic hurricane or a gentle summer rain.

5.   If you live fear, you will create fear.

6.   If you live love, you will create love.

7.   We are all creating world earth changes now as an opportunity to develop personal mastery and evolve spiritually.

8.   We must change ourselves enough that this change reflects in our societies, governments and environments. We have a conscious choice in the upcoming earth changes and that choice will help determine the outcome.

9.   This is an urgent time. The time is now!

SIMPLE IDEAS TO LIVE WITH DURING EARTH-BIRTH CHANGES

ON SURVIVAL

Feeling the best and not the worst is the only way we can survive. Are you having fun? Schedule the things you *like* to do into your life.

ON MOVING TO A SAFE PLACE

If you feel it is time to move, move *inside* first. Examine your intent carefully; are you acting with fear or love? Make the internal commitment first.

ON STORING FOOD

If you have the extra money to buy stores of food to feed your uncertain future, consider those who are in need *now*. Take your food to your local food bank.

ON COMMUNITY

If you experience a time of fear and doubts reach out to a friend, relative or neighbor. Form a group of *two or more*, and pray for the highest and best good.

FIVE MESSAGES
FOR GLOBAL CHANGE

1. Be of service, and serve by your example.

2. Be a responsible parent, not only to your own children, but to all of creation.

3. Play like children. Fill your life with joy and laughter.

4. To understand your brother or sister, develop mercy and compassion.

5. Freedom begins from unity within. The harmony and bliss of heaven radiates from this center.

NOTES

1. *Webster's New International Dictionary*, Second Edition, Unabridged, 1937.

2. *Christianity Without Religion, Sananda, Director Of Magnificent Consummation,* (Temple of The Light, 7, Santa Brigida, Gran Canaria, Spain).

3. *Solutions To Our Global Crisis,* (Causes Newsletter, New Mexico, January, 1989), Issue No. 13.

4. *Earthstar, A Treasure Map Rediscovered,* (Rosetta, Ashland, Oregon, 1991) page 1.

5. Ibid., page 2.

6. *Manly Hall, Secret Teachings Of All Ages, Pythagorean Mathematics,* (Philosophical Research Society, Inc., Los Angeles, California, 1988), page 72.

7. Ibid.

8. Ibid., *The Initiation Of The Pyramid,* page 44.

9. *Thomas Printz, The Seven Mighty Elohim Speak On The Seven Steps To Precipitation,* (The Bridge To Freedom, Inc.,1957); (Ascended Master Teaching Foundation, Mount Shasta, California, 1986), page 153.

10. *Jane Bosveld, Apocalypse, How?,* (Omni Magazine, March 1991), page 36.

11. *Keay Davidson, El Nino Strikes Again,* (Earth Magazine, Vol. 4, No. 3), Page 31.

12. *Manly Hall, Secret Teachings Of All Ages, The Elements & Their Inhabitants,* (Philosophical Research Society, Inc., Los Angeles, California, 1988), Page 108.

13. *Alexandra Wiltze, Seasons Shift As Earth Warms,* (Earth Magazine, Vol 4, #3), page 18.

14. *Jerry Canty, Eternal Massage*, (The George Ohsawa Macrobiotic Foundation, Inc. Publishers, San Francisco, California, 1971), page 41.

15. *Manly Hall, The Secret Teachings Of All Ages, Stones, Metals and Gems*, (Philosophical Research Society, Inc., Los Angeles, California, 1988), page 100.

SPECIAL THANKS

A special thank you to Jan Manzi for proof-reading this manuscript.
"Love, in service, breathes the breath for all!"

MAPS

NEW RELEASE! **FREEDOM STAR WORLD
EARTH CHANGES MAP**

The long awaited world map of earth changes prophecies. Depicts changes for Europe, Japan, Australia and the entire world. This map represents a six year study and compilation of earth changes prophecies from the Master Teachers. Gives the location of 51 sacred golden city vortexes, polar shifts, new mountains, oceans, lakes and rivers. A beautiful full color presentation, containing sacred symbols for the dawning New Age of cooperation and peace. Freedom Star is a wonderful piece of New Age art at a *very affordable* price. 36" x 52". $25 (US Funds), plus shipping and handling. (Signed and numbered prints are available on request. Laminated prints are also available. Please call for a price quote.)

I AM AMERICA MAP / DELUXE VERSION POSTER

Detailed earth changes for the United States. Poster is 28 1/2" x 22 1/2", full color and suitable for framing. THE I AM AMERICA MAP OF EARTH CHANGES is tastefully presented in full color and carries the energy and vibration of a peaceful New Age. It contains all the original information of new coastlines and the location of five prophesied Golden City Vortexes. A beautiful piece for your home. $15 (US Funds), plus shipping and handling. Shipped in a cardboard tube.

BOOKS

NEW WORLD ATLAS, VOL 1.

The perfect accompaniment to the I AM America Map containing all of the original channeled information. This book contains the Earth Changes prophecies for the United States, Canada, Mexico, Central & South America. Contains four full color mini maps and over 200 pages of detailed descriptions and spiritual guidance. Also contains the Twelve Jurisdictions. $19, plus shipping and handling. ISBN: 1-880050-01-3.

NEW WORLD ATLAS, VOL 2.

Just two days after this book was released, the Kobe earthquake struck. THIS INFORMATION IS TIMELY! This second volume of earth changes prophecies continues the message of change, as sponsored by the Ascended Masters. Beloved Kuan Yin presents earth changes prophecies for Japan, Asia and Australia as seen on Freedom Star World Map of Earth Changes. The information in this book is a must if you have read New World Atlas, Vol. 1. $17, plus shipping and handling. ISBN:1-880050-07-2.

FREEDOM STAR MANUAL

Through the use of an ancient threefold technique, Lori Adaile Toye interprets inspired earth changes prophecies for the Americas, Europe, Africa, Japan, Asia and Australia. Contains a mini-version world earth changes map, 44 pages of detailed descriptions and the location of the 51 golden cities of the planet. $9.95, plus shipping and handling. ISBN: 1-880050-04-8.

VIDEOS & AUDIOS

MOVING INTO OUR NEW WORLD VIDEO

Lori Adaile Toye presents the United States earth changes prophecies in the I hour and 15 minute video. Detailed and specific information. Perfect for centers and groups. $29.95, plus shipping and handling.

BIRTHCHANGES, by Lenard & Lori Adaile Toye

Three outstanding cassettes present timely information to lead you further on the path of mastery in the spiritual awakening.

Contained in this set are: Laws of co-creation which give you experiential tools to change your life and co-create a new world. When applied, this information leads you through the transformative journey of self to the transpersonal experience of global love and service.

Tape two, Eleven Points Of Empowering Change, presents the metaphoric and mystic message of prophecy; designed to empower you personally as a Master of Service on the path of spiritual regeneration. This is one of the most thorough and healing interpretations of earth changes prophecies ever publicly presented.

Tape three, Your Divine Being, outlines the basics of geometric language, the science of energy movement and mastery techniques for greater self-healing in the spiritual awakening. All three tapes, $24.95, plus shipping and handling.

SUPER COSMIC PHYSICS, by Lenard Toye.

A beautiful introduction on human energy fields and their relationship to individual thought, feeling and action. Lenard Toye presents his experience working as a healer with the gift of auric vision on this 60 minute cassette. If you have an interest in your own healing ability and want to know how you can help in the spiritual transition, let this information become one of your first powerful tools.

This cassette was so popular at the Global Congress that it was sold out! Lenard presents basic mystic knowledge with enthusiasm, humor and practical experience. $11.95, includes shipping and handling.

A PROPHECY OF CHOICE FOR OUR NEW WORLD by Lori Adaile Toye

Lori Adaile Toye delivers the most recent prophecies from the Ascended Masters of upcoming world earth changes. These prophecies are presented as a series of warnings that each individual can change through adopting a sensitivity of consciousness.

Also included in this cassette is a brief description of the I AM America Map, and an earth changes timeline depicting prophecies for the planet from 1992 to the year 2,660. This cassette also introduces Lori's most recent work Freedom Star, which teaches an ancient Hebraic form of interpreting prophecies. $9.95, plus shipping and handling.

JUST RELEASED! Latest Channeled Works From The Ascended Masters.

These tapes were received via trance channeling and have been kept in the authentic condition. There have been no alterations to the sound quality so each listener may receive full benefit of the vibrational energy of trance work and its healing effect.

TEACHINGS ON SPIRITUAL FREEDOM

Saint Germain, Sananda, Kuan Yin, Mary. Received through Lori Adaile Toye, May 1993.

Simple, yet beautiful teachings that lead us into the Age of Spiritual Freedom. This channeled work brings the wisdom and healing energy of four of the best known spiritual leaders and teachers in humanity's history. $9.95, plus shipping and handling.

THE COURAGE TO HEAL

Saint Germain and Sananda, received through Lori Adaile Toye, June 1993.

Contains a complete outline on the purpose of natural law and the three Ascended Master laws that lead the chela to adeptship. $9.95, plus shipping and handling.

FREEDOM MESSAGE / THE GARDEN /
TEACHINGS OF ONENESS

Saint Germain, Sananda, Mary, Archangel Crystiel. Received through Lori Adaile and Lenard Toye, July 1993.

Beloved Saint Germain sends a call throughout the world to expand the aggregate body of light. In our freedom of service we learn of our destiny to serve, known as the Law Of Form. Also, a beautiful meditation with Sananda in the infinite garden of the one life (Monad) and teachings of healership as participating consciousness.

The second tape introduces the teaching of the mighty one, the Monad. Known as teachings of the eighth octave, Archangel Crystiel delivers a message of one with perfection with the perfection of ONE. $11.95, two tapes, plus shipping and handling.

THE SHERRY TAPE / Teachings On Immortality

Saint Germain, received through Lori Adaile Toye, August, 1993.

Some of the most outstanding information on immortality is contained on this tape. Named after our dear friend, Sherry Takala, The Sherry Tape was originally her personal reading with beloved Saint Germain. Due to the nature of this timely message, we decided to release this tape. Remember, this recording is very authentic, (dogs bark and doors slam), please overlook this and receive some of the most thought provoking channeled material to date. $9.95, plus shipping and handling.

EARTH HEALING / FORGIVENESS

Bend, Oregon, June 22, 1994. Received through Lori Adaile Toye.

Side A: A beautiful discourse, received in ceremony, Saint Germain gives guidance on the healing of the planet through the vehicle of choice. Side B: The law of forgiveness and the use of the violet flame. $9.95, plus shipping and handling.

IMMORTALITY OF CONSCIOUSNESS / SHAMBALLA

Asotin, Washington, New Year's Eve, 1993. Received through Lori Adaile Toye.

Side A: Saint Germain addresses levels of conscious immortality and their relationship to physical immortality. Side B: A celebration at Shamballa and an invitation to join in the joy of perfect life. $9.95, plus shipping and handling.

☞ TO ORDER SEE NEXT PAGE

I AM AMERICA

P.O. Box 2511 Payson AZ 85547
PHONE ORDERS: 1-520-474-1341 Or

Toll Free: 1-800-930-1341

or FAX Your Order: FAX# (520) 474-8799
FOR CUSTOMER SERVICE: (520) 474-3060

NAME_____

ADDRESS_____PHONE (   )_____

CITY_____STATE_____ZIP_____

____CHECK ____MONEY ORDER ____COD, Shipped UPS only, add $5 to order.

____ [MasterCard] ____ [VISA] Card #_____ EXP Date_____

Signature_____

SHIPPING & HANDLING

IF SUBTOTAL IS:	CONTINENTAL U.S.	AK & HI
From $.00 to $15.00	$3.95	$6.95
From $15.01 to $35.00	$5.95	$8.95
From $35.01 to $55.00	$6.95	$11.95
From $55.01 to $75.00	$7.95	$12.95
From $75.01 to $110.00	$7.95	$15.95
From $110.01 to $210.00	$8.95	$16.95
From $210.01 to $300.00	$10.45	$17.95
Over 301.01	$10.95	$18.95

Next day air shipping by phone orders only.

CANADIAN ORDERS IF SUBTOTAL IS:

From $1.00 to $25.00 Add $5.00
From $25.01 to $50.00 Add $8.00
From $50.01 to $100.00 Add $12.00
From $100.01 to $200.00 Add $17.00
For each additional $100.00 spent, please include an extra $17.00.

Please include regular shipping from Continental United States Column plus handling fees and additional charges below. ALL FOREIGN ORDERS, (Except Canada), CALL FOR A PRICE QUOTE.

ITEM / DESCRIPTION	HOW MANY	UNIT PRICE	TOTAL PRICE
		SUBTOTAL	

Please use Credit Card or send U.S. FUNDS drawn on a U.S. Bank only. *We do not ship to Mexico, Central America or South America by Postal Services. We can ship to authorized UPS zones, call for a quotation.*	*Arizona Residents Add 6.7% Sales Tax*	
	SHIPPING & HANDLING	
	FOREIGN ORDER FEE (IF APPLICABLE)	
ALLOW 4-6 WEEKS FOR DELIVERY.	**NET TOTAL**	

ALL ORDERS SHIPPED U.S. POSTAL SERVICE & UPS
Overnight & 2 day service are available through UPS. Call for price quote.